Coach Mom
Top College Admission Playbook
How to Stand Out and Get into Dream Schools

Elizabeth Gardner

© 2021 Elizabeth Anne Gardner All rights reserved.
ISBN-13: 979-8-588-11943-6

No portion of this book may be reproduced in any form without permission from the author, except as permitted by U.S. copyright law. The author and publisher hereby disclaim and do not assume liability for any injury, loss, damage, or disruption caused by errors or omissions in this book, regardless of whether errors or omissions result from negligence, accident, or any other cause. For rights and permissions, please contact: Elizabeth Gardner neonpinklime@gmail.com

Contents

Chapter One Pep Talk 1

Chapter Two A Clear Understanding of the College Admission Process 3

Chapter Three What to Do in Middle School 5

Chapter Four What to Do in High School 9

Chapter Five How to Maintain a High GPA 29

Chapter Six SAT, ACT, SAT II and Test Optional 34

Chapter Seven A Spiky Ball Extracurricular Activities 41

Chapter Eight You Can Afford It Need Blind vs Meet Full Need Colleges 48

Chapter Nine Early vs. Regular Decision: Target a Specific College 52

Chapter Ten College Admission Rules to Break 58

Chapter Eleven Essay Brainstorming and Writing 60

Chapter Twelve Create a Narrative to Focus Your Application ... 77

Chapter Thirteen Make the Most of Each Application Section 81

Chapter Fourteen Admission Don'ts 95

Chapter Fifteen Contacting Admissions: Mistakes, Interviews, Deferrals, Waitlists and LOCIs 100

Chapter Sixteen Application Disasters 105

Help People Like You Beat the System! 109

About the Author 110

Chapter One

Pep Talk

"I used a random number generator to select which college to open first," Lauren nervously explained. It was Ivy Day. *"First up is Princeton,"* she said. *Our family formed a semicircle around her and steeled ourselves for almost certain disappointment. Lauren summoned her courage. "Here goes." She clicked 'status update.' An orange tiger head popped up with "Congratulations!" beneath. "W-W-What?" Lauren stammered. Euphoric cheers and astonished gasps rang out. Her official acceptance letter read, "Congratulations! On behalf of my colleagues in Morrison Hall, I am thrilled to offer you admission to Princeton. Your accomplishments inside and outside of the classroom stood out in a highly competitive pool..."*

To get in you have to stand out. Each year top colleges receive tens of thousands of applications with high grades and standardized test scores. How do they choose? Admission officers look for personality and pursuits that stick out. Think of it this way: Excellent grades and test scores qualify you for consideration, but it's your pursuits and personality articulated through thoughtfully crafted essays that get you in.

Hello. My name is Elizabeth Gardner, and I've been coaching my kids Eiche ("Ike"), Max, and Lauren through the college admission process since 2008. Our family couldn't afford tutors, college admission consultants, or ACT/SAT prep courses, so we did it ourselves. Over the past thirteen years, I've spent hundreds of hours studying online sources including admission forums and blogs, admission dean and officer interviews, essay writing sites, college admission consultant videos, college websites, ACT/SAT forums, and financial aid sites.

With a 3-6% regular decision admit rate, it's extremely difficult to get into elite universities. As a coach, I've got a pretty good track record. Between them, my kids were admitted to: University of Kentucky, University of South Carolina, North Carolina State University, Clemson University, University of North Carolina Chapel Hill, Pennsylvania State University, Virginia Tech, Davidson College, University of Virginia, Duke University, and Princeton University.

Yes, you can get in! Yes, you can afford it! Getting admitted to Ivy level colleges requires a clear understanding of the process, organization, strategy, determination, inspiration, and years of hard work. Using examples from successful college applications to explain application strategy, *Coach Mom Top College Admission Playbook* is perfect for the high school applicant or parent coach. As you aim for dream schools, keep in mind that the most important qualities they seek are authenticity and integrity. Shoot for the stars by being yourself in your applications. Don't copy someone else's work or change your essays to please a parent, teacher, or anyone else.

Chapter Two

A Clear Understanding of the College Admission Process

"Wait. So, why do I have to work on my college essays now? It's only June." Skeptical, Eiche was eager to return to video games. "Look." I pointed to my laptop. He leaned in to see. "Oh crap. NC State's early application is due in October? Are they all like that?" He balked. "No," I explained. "Most are due November 1st, but you won't have time to write all these essays once you're back in school."

Students apply to college during their senior year of high school. Most early applications are due November 1st with admission decisions released around December 15th. Most regular decision applications are due January 1st with decisions in late March. Consult college websites for exact dates. There are advantages to applying early. Please refer to the "Early vs. Regular Decision" chapter for an in-depth discussion of early versus regular decision strategy. Most applicants use either the Common Application or the Coalition Application to apply. The Common Application is the most popular and accepted by over 900 schools.

The best time to write college applications and essays is the summer between junior and senior years when you'll have time to devote. For more, see the "What to do in High School" chapter which lists steps to take freshman, sophomore, junior, and senior years toward your college admission goals. To fill out your Common Application, see the "Make the Most of Each Application Section" chapter. And for help writing your college essays, see the "Essay Brainstorming and Writing" chapter.

How Top Colleges Evaluate Applications
In order of importance, holistic review

1. Authenticity and Integrity
2. High School Transcript Challenging Curriculum – high grades predict college success
3. ACT/SAT – high scores show aptitude
4. Extracurricular Activities
5. Letters of Recommendation High School Counselor/Teachers
6. Essays
7. Diversity – economic, geographic, ethnic, gender

College admission officers consider the high school transcript the best indicator of success in college; therefore, it's one of the most important factors for applicants. Standardized test scores are next in importance. Top colleges receive thousands of applications per admission cycle with high school transcripts that use different grading scales. Admissions relies on standardized test scores from the ACT or SAT as a way to objectively assess academic aptitude. The rest of the factors like extracurricular activities, letters of recommendation, essays, and diversity (economic, geographic, ethnic, gender) complete admission's "holistic review" process. Holistic review means that admissions will consider all of an applicant's characteristics and how those characteristics could contribute to their university's learning community.

Chapter Three

What to Do in Middle School

"Where's Max?" I quickly started our minivan and buckled my seatbelt. We were already ten minutes late. "He ran inside to get his backpack," Lauren replied. I handed her a metal case of DVDs. "Throw this in the back. It doesn't belong up here." She flung the case over her shoulder. Max returned, opened the van door, and cried out, "What happened to my ship?!" I turned and gasped. His hand-crafted, paper model of space shuttle Challenger lay crushed beneath the metal case.

It's your abilities and pursuits that will propel your future college applications. Middle school is a time of discovery. Explore as many of your interests as possible, and try not to let life's hectic pace crush your dreams along the way.

Please refer to the "How Top Colleges Evaluate Applications" list on the prior page. Focus on grades and activities during middle school. The rest of the list you can't do much about until high school. Regarding diversity, e.g., how much your family makes, where you live, your gender and ethnicity, it's not something that can be changed for the most part; fortunately, colleges are looking for students from all ethnic, geographic, and economic backgrounds.

Use middle school as a trial run for high school.

Why do high school grades matter so much to colleges? Because they're the best predictor of how applicants will do in college. Use middle school as a trial run to see what kind of grades you can maintain. Since colleges won't see middle school grades, you can take honors or accelerated classes without fear of a low grade marring your transcript. Consider the following five questions.

- Do you get A, B, or C grades or a combination?
- Can you maintain mostly A grades without undue stress?
- How do you feel about the pressure? Can you maintain happiness?
- If you can't do it here, then *will* you in high school?
- If you can do it here, then will you *want* to do it in high school?

Parents, talk with your kids about coaching them on their college admission journey. Discuss these questions. Listen carefully to what they say. Do they want to shoot for Ivy League level colleges? Not every kid wants to go to college, and even among those who do many are not able to maintain an A average. Please see the "How to Maintain a High GPA" chapter for a full discussion of how high grades need to be to get into elite universities. Adjust your expectations to your son or daughter's enthusiasm and ability. In other words, love and support them for who they are. Ivy level colleges may not be for them. There are plenty of other good universities, and the college admission strategies in this book will be effective getting them in anywhere they choose.

Take advanced classes in middle school.

When colleges examine an applicant's high school transcript, they look for applicants that challenged themselves by taking the most difficult courses their high school offers. They are even more impressed when students go beyond their high school's curriculum by taking courses at local or community colleges. Taking advanced/accelerated middle school courses will satisfy high school prerequisites and create more room in your high school schedule for AP, IB, or other advanced courses. Most middle schools have advanced or accelerated classes in foreign language, math, and English.

My kids Eiche, Max, and Lauren, for example, were on the accelerated math track in middle school. That allowed them to start advanced math freshman year of high school and complete calculus by the end of their junior year. During junior year, Eiche and Lauren went beyond their high school's curriculum by taking calculus at a local college, and Max took it online. Additionally, taking advanced math in middle school allowed them more room in their schedules for AP courses and advanced electives. And for Eiche and Max, taking calculus junior year was necessary for their early applications to engineering colleges. Early college applications typically include only first quarter senior year grades.

Middle school activities can help you discover what you truly love to do.

As we've discussed, admission officers sort through thousands of applications to find applicants whose character and pursuits stick out. How an applicant spends their free time reveals a lot about them. It's one of the ways colleges will get to know you through your application. Think about it this way—good grades and standardized test scores qualify you for consideration, but you'll need something extra like a hobby or other activity to make you stand out among a sea of similarly qualified candidates. Middle school is a fun, low stress time to begin figuring out your likes and dislikes by trying different activities. What you're looking for are one or two (or more) that you'll love and stick with through high school.

Stumped? Consider birthday and holiday gifts you've received. I'm not talking about video games, phones, or tv's, but rather things that met your specific interests like, for example, telescope, chemistry set, paints, crafting materials, sewing machine, microscope, butterfly net, fish tank, etc. These are the kinds of pursuits that can turn into a passion now that could last through high school. Or, what about trying something new that you've always wanted to try? Search the Web to show you how.

That's what my kids did, and it started during middle school. Both Max and his younger sister Lauren showed an early interest in art. Max made his own comic books and created intricate origami using YouTube. Lauren also relied on YouTube to teach her to draw and paint. She joined Max in making origami but was more obsessed with making backpacks, patches, jewelry, t-shirts, and hummingbird swings. One summer, Lauren helped Max make an elaborate dollhouse with furniture completely out of paper. During middle and high school, Max constructed paper spaceships including space shuttles. He was so consumed by intricate detail that he even made tiny paper satellites to put in the space shuttle cargo bays! In high school, Lauren focused on watercolor painting and graphite. Between junior and senior year, she painted a climate change inspired, watercolor portfolio entitled "Metanoia" for the Scholastic Art awards competition that was also featured at her high school's "Night of the Arts" community showcase. As their different interests evolved over time, our family cheered them on and provided financial support when possible. Their passion for projects came from within them. Once they found something they loved, they ran with it.

Whatever you discover, be it a hobby, writing, art, academic club, sports, community service, research project, or some other fascinating pursuit, ask your parents for encouragement and support. Drop activities you're not passionate about and move on to ones you love. Authenticity. And while you're figuring out what you love to do, try to find at least one pursuit that's atypical or unusual. Maybe something that reflects the unique culture of your local area, or an unusual interest that reflects your personality or a quirk? This is known as your "spike" and could eventually help you stick out from thousands of similarly qualified candidates. See "A Spiky Ball" chapter for more help finding your spike.

Chapter Four

What to Do in High School

Inspired by tumbling on the TV show "Dance Moms" during grade school, Lauren taught herself a back handspring using a mattress and YouTube. She joined her middle school cheer team with dreams of high school cheer and then disaster struck! Lauren hyperextended her knee playing soccer and was unable to tryout for varsity cheer. "Mom, did you video any of my tumbling at middle school games?" Lauren submitted a video and made the varsity cheer squad freshman year. She liked soccer but loved cheer, so she dropped soccer.

As you began thinking about and working toward your college goals in middle school, you developed study skills to maintain high grades and explored extracurriculars. High school is where that process of personal accomplishment and discovery deepens.

How Top Colleges Evaluate Applications
In order of importance, holistic review

1. Authenticity and Integrity
2. High School Transcript Challenging Curriculum – high grades predict college success
3. ACT/SAT – high scores show aptitude
4. Extracurricular Activities
5. Letters of Recommendation High School Counselor/Teachers
6. Essays
7. Diversity – economic, geographic, ethnic, gender

College admission officers consider the high school transcript the best indicator of success in college; therefore, it's one of the most important factors for applicants. Standardized test scores are next in importance. Top colleges receive thousands of applications per admission cycle with high school transcripts that use different grading scales. Admissions relies on standardized test scores from the ACT or SAT as a way to objectively assess academic aptitude. The rest of the factors like extracurricular activities, letters of recommendation, essays, and diversity (economic, geographic, ethnic, gender) complete admission's "holistic review" process. Holistic review means that admissions will consider all of an applicant's characteristics and how those characteristics could contribute to their university's learning community.

Use the "How Top Colleges Evaluate Applications" list as a general guide to where to focus your time during high school. The rest of this chapter provides a list of specific steps to take each year.

FRESHMAN YEAR

1. Focus on curriculum and extracurricular activities.

2. Curriculum: Colleges want to see a curriculum that challenges you.

- **Get the highest grades possible.** See "How to Maintain a High GPA" chapter.
- **Take the most challenging curriculum your school has to offer.** When colleges examine an applicant's high school transcript, they look for applicants that challenged themselves by taking the most difficult courses their high school offers. They are even more impressed when students go beyond their high school's curriculum by taking courses at local or community colleges. If your high school doesn't have AP or only a few, take those and then seek dual enrollment courses at community colleges, local colleges, or online. If your high school has AP, IB or another advanced curriculum, take as much as you can to create a challenging schedule.
- **Take courses beyond your high school's curriculum if possible**, e.g., dual enrollment at community colleges, local colleges, or online.
- **Balance curriculum difficulty and grades.** Get the best grades possible while still challenging yourself, but don't overload.

3. Activities:

- **Continue middle school activities if you enjoy them,** and see what high school academic clubs, varsity sports, or competitive academic teams interest you.
- **It's best to have both solo and team activities to demonstrate you can work well alone or in a group.** Start thinking about where and how to eventually show leadership in these activities.

- **Try to find an activity or hobby that will be unusual and make you stick out from the crowd.** Quit activities you aren't passionate about and try something else. To be authentic, you need to love what you do.
- **Well-rounded vs. one or two activities you're passionate about?** You want to be well-rounded like a ball but with an unusual or specialist activity spike. Please see "A Spiky Ball" chapter.
- **State/national/global recognition?** Ivy league caliber schools look for this in applications. See strategies in "A Spiky Ball" chapter for more.

4. Spend time getting to know your guidance counselor. They will write a college recommendation that's more meaningful and impactful if they know you.

5. Save your work for college application portfolio(s). College application portfolios are optional, so most applicants don't include one. That's a mistake. A portfolio showcases your talent and growth over time making it a great way to stand out among applicants. You'll be able to create one or more portfolios using the Common Application when you apply. Types of portfolios include (but are not limited to) art, music, scientific research (published and unpublished), novels, poetry, news articles, screenplays, performance (vocal, solo, choral, musical instrument, comedy theatre, storytelling), photography, videos, crafting, and building. Each year of high school starting freshman year, save things you create or do for a future college application portfolio(s). See the "Make the Most of Each Application Section" chapter for more about creating an application portfolio.

6. Summer between freshman and sophomore year

- **Look for summer activities and/or local camps that relate to your interests.**
- **Travel opportunities or college hosted camps?** Fine if you can afford them; however, a top college's summer program will not help you get into that particular college.

These programs are unrelated to admissions and are revenue generators for colleges, but it's a nice way to visit campuses.

- **Summer jobs are a good choice.** Working as a babysitter, pet sitter, mowing lawns, picking up groceries, etc., are wonderful character-building activities that show leadership, hard work, determination, and provide plenty of interesting stories for long/short college application essays. Besides, if you need money let colleges see that you worked hard for it. Economic Diversity.
- **Community service:** Most colleges like to see some community involvement; therefore, it's a good idea to do some but it doesn't have to be a big commitment. For a full discussion of community service, see "A Spiky Ball" chapter.
- **Study for the ACT or SAT using old exams under timed conditions.** At the end of the summer, register to take the ACT or SAT (full test) at the start of your sophomore year to establish a baseline of your ability for future studying. This test is meant to give you experience taking the exam. You'll learn what test sections you need to focus on for next summer. See the "SAT, ACT, SAT II and Test Optional" chapter for more.

SOPHOMORE YEAR

1. **Focus on curriculum and extracurricular activities.**

2. **Curriculum:** Colleges want to see a curriculum that challenges you.

- **Get the highest grades possible.** See "How to Maintain a High GPA" chapter.
- **When colleges examine an applicant's high school transcript, they look for applicants that challenged themselves by taking the most difficult courses their high school offers.** They are even more impressed when students go beyond their high school's curriculum by taking courses at local or community colleges. Take the most challenging curriculum your school has to offer. If your high school doesn't have AP or only a few, take those and then seek dual enrollment courses at community colleges, local colleges, or online. If your high school has AP, IB or another advanced curriculum, take as much as you can to create a challenging schedule.
- **Take courses beyond your high school's curriculum if possible**, e.g., dual enrollment at community colleges, local colleges, or online.
- **Balancing act: get the best grades possible while still challenging yourself.** Don't overload.

3. Activities.

- **Continue looking for activities and/or stick to ones you've got plus look for leadership opportunities to pursue within those activities.** Keep your eyes open. Sometimes while pursuing one activity something even more interesting or unusual will pop up. It's time to decide what you want to do with your extra time and stick to it. You have only two more years to devote to activities before college applications are due. Make sure that it's something you love and excel at.

- **Last chance to find a hobby or extracurricular or community service that's specialist or unusual.** Something that will make you stick out from the crowd, i.e., a spike. If you already have a hobby or extracurricular activity or community service that's unusual, then continue that. Otherwise, find one that you can spend at least two years pursuing. Please see "A Spiky Ball" chapter for an in-depth discussion about finding your spike.

4. Take the ACT or SAT exam that you scheduled over the summer. Use your score as a baseline for studying the following summer. PSAT and PreACT tests may be accurate predictors of what you'll score on the actual exam, but it's more valuable to have the real experience and scores of an actual exam. Please see the "SAT, ACT, SAT II and Test Optional" chapter.

5. Continue getting to know your guidance counselor.

6. Summer between sophomore and junior year

- **Study old ACT or SAT exams in preparation for taking the exam once or twice (if necessary) junior year.** Focus on the sections of the exam that give you the most trouble. Please see the "SAT, ACT, SAT II and Test Optional" chapter.
- **Visit colleges you want to apply to. Start to decide where to apply.** For help deciding where to go, see the "You Can Afford It. Need Blind vs. Meet Full Need Colleges" chapter.
- **Pursue interesting camps or other activities.** They don't have to be long commitments or even an entire summer. For example, Lauren attended a week-long summer camp held by her county fixing hiking trails and cleaning streams. Eiche and Max volunteered at a community thrift store. Please see "A Spiky Ball" chapter for extracurricular activity possibilities.
- **Summer jobs are always a good choice.** If you need to work then do so. That's who you are. Authenticity. Economic diversity. If you're sixteen there are lots of

places to work. These experiences will provide meaningful material for college application essays.
- **At the end of the summer before beginning junior year, register to take the ACT or SAT early your junior year.**

JUNIOR YEAR

1. Focus on curriculum and extracurricular activities.

2. Curriculum: Colleges want to see a curriculum that challenges you.

- **Get the highest grades possible.** See "How to Maintain a High GPA" chapter.
- **When colleges examine an applicant's high school transcript, they look for applicants that challenged themselves by taking the most difficult courses their high school offers.** They are even more impressed when students go beyond their high school's curriculum by taking courses at local or community colleges. Take the most challenging curriculum your school has to offer. If your high school doesn't have AP or only a few, take those and then seek dual enrollment courses at community colleges, local colleges, or online. If your high school has AP, IB or another advanced curriculum, take as much as you can to create a challenging schedule.
- **Take courses beyond your high school's curriculum if possible**, e.g., dual enrollment at community colleges, local colleges, or online.
- **Balancing act: get the best grades possible while still challenging yourself.** Don't overload.

3. Activities

- **There should be an opportunity to demonstrate leadership in one or more of your activities junior year.** For example, captain of the high school soccer team or captain of the varsity cheer squad, tutoring other students, leadership in martial arts, canvassing for political candidates, leading the school debate team, etc.
- **Starting new activities is fine, and you can drop activities if you want.** Explain abrupt changes in your college application's Additional Information section. If you don't want to do an activity anymore and want to try

something else then say so. Authenticity. Just remember it's good to have one or two long-term activities demonstrating that you have the tenacity and determination to pursue interests and long-term goals. Please see "A Spiky Ball" chapter for extracurricular activity possibilities.

4. Take the ACT or SAT at the earliest possible date after summer studying. Get a fee waiver from your guidance counselor if you qualify. If you're unhappy with your test scores, retake prior to the end of junior year. Do not register to take the exam senior year unless you have to. Your summer between junior and senior year will be busy with writing college applications and essays. See the "SAT, ACT, SAT II and Test Optional" chapter.

5. Take high school courses that help you figure out what you want to study in college, and what you don't. For example, if you're good at math and science, then perhaps you'd like to be an engineer? If so, take honors or AP Physics to see if you like it. If you want to be a writer or journalist, perhaps you should take high-level writing and civics courses? You'll discover whether you like those subjects enough to spend tuition money on them in college. As you figure out what you like in high school, you'll take more courses on it and your transcript will thereby reflect your interests which will help reinforce your college application narrative (story). See "Create a Narrative to Focus Your Application" chapter for more.

6. Get to know your teachers and start thinking about who could write good recommendations for your college applications.

7. Write a one-page resume.

- **You'll need this for guidance counselor and teacher recommendations, scholarship applications, college interviews, and for reference when you fill out the honors and activities sections of your college applications.** If you already have a resume, edit it so it is up to date.

- **It should contain name, address, email, phone number. Sections Titles: Education, Honors, Activities, Employment, Community Service.** Google "resume" for examples.
- **Create a "College Applications" folder on your computer to store everything relating to college admissions.** Create a subfolder called "resume". Keep all versions of your resume in the subfolder by saving under new versions like v1, v2, etc. It's important to keep versions to help prevent accidentally deleting vital information.

8. At the end of junior year, ask two teachers for written recommendations for senior year.

- **They should be teachers who know you well.** Ask for a good recommendation. If they hesitate or say no then find someone else.
- **Why ask them before senior year?** Because sometimes teachers limit the number of recommendations they'll write, so if you ask early, you're more likely to get the teachers you want. When you return to school in the fall remind them.
- **Create a subfolder in your "College Applications" folder called "recommendations".** Keep cover letters asking for teacher recommendations.

9. Ask your guidance counselor for a list of available university scholarships. Colleges contact high schools and provide them opportunities to nominate top students for scholarships. If you're interested in being nominated or receiving scholarship applications, let your guidance counselor know by the end of junior year so that you can receive a nomination or apply early senior year. Sometimes there's a limit to the number of students that can be nominated.

10. Summer between junior and senior year

- **Continue with summer activities of past summers.** Start something new if you feel inspired, but remember this will be a busy summer of college essay writing with little free time.
- **If you're happy with your ACT/SAT score, no need to study for this.** If you want to try again, you'll have to budget time for test prep. Colleges don't like more than three testings because they'd rather you use your time more productively, e.g., on your interests. Don't forget to schedule a date to take the exam. See the "SAT, ACT, SAT II and Test Optional" chapter.
- **Create your college list. Make sure it's a well-balanced list, i.e., some reach, some middle, some safety schools.** For help deciding where to apply, see the "You Can Afford It. Need Blind vs. Meet Full Need Colleges" chapter. For what you need to know about applying early, regular decision, and safety schools, please see the "Early vs. Regular Decision" chapter. Decide which colleges you will apply early, e.g., early action (EA), early decision (ED), restricted early action (REA), or single choice early action (SCEA), and which to apply regular decision (RD). Google your chances of admission to each school by searching average ACT/SAT score, GPA, and percentage of students admitted EA, ED, REA, SCEA versus RD. Create a subfolder on your computer under your "College Applications" folder for each college to help you stay organized. Keep essays for each college in their folder. Save all drafts with version numbers. This is particularly important when working on essays because you may decide to go back to early versions for prior information and inspiration.
- **Create a new email address to use solely for college admissions.** You'll be receiving a ton of college application related email. Having one email account for all correspondence, e.g., ACT/SAT score report orders, transcript orders, request for teacher recommendations, guidance counselor correspondence, and college

admissions correspondence, will reduce confusion and help you stay organized. College admission officers will be seeing this email address on your applications and correspondence, so pick something appropriate.
- **If eligible, join college admission programs that will increase your chance of admission to competitive colleges for low-income (sometimes middle income) and/or first-generation college students.** Programs such as QuestBridge and Leadership Enterprise for a Diverse America (LEDA) can give you a higher profile thereby increasing your chance of admission. Follow the directions on their websites to apply. Please see "A Spiky Ball" chapter for more information.
- **Visit college websites and learn about the schools you want to apply to.** Learn from their undergraduate office of admission page what kind of students they're looking for. Go to YouTube and search for interviews with admission officers and listen to what they say. Different schools are looking for different qualities. Some value leadership more than community service for example. This information will help guide what to emphasize in your application and more specifically in your essays. Please see "Early vs. Regular Admission - Target Specific Schools" chapter for more information. Double check admission requirements and make sure you've taken the high school classes and standardized tests they require; however, if you have not this is not necessarily a deal breaker. See full discussion in chapter "College Admission Rules to Break."
- **Create an account for the Common Application (or the Coalition Application) using the new email address you just created.** Make sure that the application you decide to use is also used by the colleges to which you want to apply. Most colleges accept the Common Application. Less accept the Coalition Application. Some accept both. Some accept neither and have their own application on their website.
- **Write all your college application due dates for early and regular decisions on a wall calendar to keep track.** There's also a calendar in your Common Application dashboard that can help you keep track.

- **In your application, start working on the activities and honors sections.** If you created a resume, this will help. If you haven't created a resume yet, then filling out the honors and activities sections will help you create one. You'll need a resume for scholarship applications in the coming months anyway. Finish the activities and honors sections before high school resumes in the fall. You'll have the chance to tweak it over the summer and into the fall, but have it basically done before you go back for senior year. Once your school work and activities start, there will not be much time to work on college applications. Please see chapter "Make the Most of Each Application Section" for a complete discussion of honors and activities sections strategies.
- **Write your college essays.** Complete the main essay for the Common Application first. Work on supplement essays for early applications next. If you have time toward the end of the summer, write regular decision essays. Write as many of them as you can before high school resumes. These take a great deal of time because of the amount of introspection and drafts required. The essays are the most important part of your application because it's your chance to speak directly to the admission committee in your own voice. Review, edit, polish essays, and then walk away for a while. Pick them up to review and polish during the first few weeks of high school. For in depth discussion of how to write your essays, see the "Essay Brainstorming and Writing" chapter.
- **Visit as many college campuses on your list as you can and get a feel for the energy and culture of campus.** Visit cafeterias, libraries, recreational areas, and dorms. Walk the neighborhoods around the school as well. I don't recommend guided tours. We got more out of walking around with map in hand. Memorably, Lauren guided us on a "coffee tour" of Duke University. And Eiche guided us to cafeterias and libraries at Virginia Tech, Clemson, and the University of Virginia.

SENIOR YEAR

1. Continue focus on grades and activities.

2. Keep a calendar to keep track of college application due dates.

3. If you're taking the ACT/SAT, make sure you take it early enough that your scores are available for Early Action (EA), Early Decision (ED), Restricted Early Action (REA), and Single Choice Early Action (SCEA). See chapter "Early vs. Regular Decision" for more on applying early.

4. Ask your guidance counselor for fee waivers for ACT or SAT score reports and college application fees if you're eligible.

5. Scholarships. If the colleges you're applying to offer scholarships, then follow their rules and apply. Check their websites for scholarship opportunities and applications. Check with your guidance counselor to see if your high school has a nomination process or other scholarship applications.

6. All college applications require a guidance counselor recommendation. Talk to your counselor about yours. Give them your resume and discuss possible topics to write about. If you have anything that you'd like them to mention in the recommendation, ask them to do that. See "Make the Most of Each Application Section" chapter for a discussion of guidance counselor and teacher recommendation strategies. Login to your common application portal and send them a recommendation request.

7. A month prior to college applications due dates, calendar order dates for ACT/SAT score reports and academic transcripts from dual enrollment, community colleges, and other colleges that you attended during high school. When those dates come up, order the score reports and transcripts. Why so early? They typically take two weeks to arrive, and you'll need time to chase them down if they don't. Once they're ordered, calendar a date two weeks later to check on the score reports and transcripts to make sure they've arrived. There's a lot to keep track of, so I suggest using a manilla folder for transcripts/ACT/SAT receipts and copies of email confirmations. You can also jot down notes in the folder if you have to chase transcripts or score reports. Write down contact dates, so you can track your follow-up calls. If you don't receive confirmation of receipt by two weeks before the application is due, call ACT/SAT/dual enrollment college and request verification that the report has been sent.

8. Remind teachers who agreed to write recommendations that it's time. Log into your Common Application portal and send them recommendation requests. Traditionally, students provide a resume and high school transcript along with a cover letter for each teacher writing a recommendation. In the cover letter, emphasize that college admissions want to know what you're like in the classroom by telling meaningful stories that demonstrate your personality, curiosity, and contributions to class discussion. At large or private high schools where the faculty has experience writing recommendations, they may know this already. However, if you attend a small or rural high school, they may not. Additionally, consider submitting an optional recommendation from someone in the community if the college you're applying to allows it. These can provide powerful character testimonials and will help your application stand out. See "Make the Most of Each Application Section" chapter for a discussion of guidance counselor and teacher recommendation strategies.

9. Give your college essays to someone you trust to review for grammar and spelling errors. Your mom, dad, or a teacher. Ask one or two people to review your work but not more. Listen to their opinions and suggestions but remember it's important that your essays reflect you and no one else. Authenticity. Do not change an essay you're happy with to please someone else.

10. Finish your applications. Double check your Common Application portal to confirm that all recommendations have been received. If any are missing, contact the missing teachers or guidance counselor until their recommendation is received. Submit your application at least a week or few days prior to the due date. You don't want to wait until the day it's due or even the day before because of the chance of technical problems or unforeseen circumstances that could've been solved if you'd submitted it days or a week before. Early applications are generally due November 1, but some are due mid-September and mid-October. Use your calendar and the calendar in the dashboard of the Common Application to keep track. See the "Make the Most of Each Application Section" chapter to make sure you've gotten the most out of your application. Also, review the "Admission Don'ts" chapter as well as the "College Admissions Rules to Break" chapter for extra tips before you submit.

11. Time to submit your application. Read through the entire application including supplements using the PDF review feature in the Common Application. The PDF view is essential because it will show you exactly how your application will look when admission officers review it. Once you submit your application it cannot be changed, so make sure it's exactly the way you want it. Some supplements must be submitted separately. Portfolios also must be submitted separately. Make sure that you've submitted every part of your application.

12. Create a manila folder for each college to which you apply. When you apply, print out a copy of the application and the submission receipt and put it in the folder. A copy will also be available in PDF form in the Common Application, and it's a good idea to save that too. It's nice to see what your application looks like in printed form, and it's handy to have the printed version for reference. And you might need it due to deletion or other problem.

13. After application submission, each college will email you a link to their admission portal with username and password. Usually, your username is your email address. It will take a few days for this information to arrive, up to a week. Colleges are busy receiving thousands of applications, so be patient. Once you log in to each college's applicant portal, you'll see a list of items that are not yet received or checked off. As the college receives ACT/SAT scores, transcripts, recommendations, art portfolio, FAFSA and so forth those items will be checked off the list. Monitor this list and contact admissions and/or financial aid offices if items are not checked off after a reasonable time.

14. After you submit your college application, start working on your financial aid application. Check your colleges' deadlines for the Free Application for Student Aid (FAFSA) and the College Scholarship Service Profile (CSS Profile) which are due early for early college applications. Early college applications are due on or around November 1, so the FAFSA and CSS Profile are typically due a week or two later. If you're late submitting the FAFSA and CSS Profile, then you won't receive your financial aid offer with your acceptance on or about December 1-15 for early applications and late March for regular decision applications. You'll need a copy of your parents' prior, prior year tax return for reference when filling out these financial aid applications. FAFSA will tell you what year to use. Create a manilla folder for the FAFSA & CSS Profile. When you create an account on the FAFSA website, the federal government will email you a FAFSA ID and you create the password.

When you finish filing the FAFSA, print out a copy and keep it in the file with any notes you need so that you can log back in. When you complete a FAFSA, you need only one copy because each college you apply to will receive their own copy of your FAFSA automatically. Each college has a different due date for receiving their copy of your FAFSA. Make sure you've completed the FAFSA and added colleges to your FAFSA list prior to that college's FAFSA deadline. In addition, most colleges require a CSS Profile or their own financial aid application. The CSS Profile and university specific financial aid applications go more in depth about your finances than the FAFSA does. When you complete a CSS Profile, you only need one copy because you'll list on it all the schools you're applying to and they will automatically receive the same copy (just like with the FAFSA). Print a copy of your CSS profile and put it in your FAFSA CSS Profile folder. A few universities require their own financial aid application. Once done, print a copy and put it in that college's file. It's useful to have a copy of your FAFSA application for reference when you fill out the CSS Profile or university financial aid application because many of the questions are similar.

15. A few weeks after you submit your college applications, colleges will contact you to schedule interviews with local alumni. Do not ignore or refuse interviews. If you do, you'll most likely not be admitted. The interviews are generally low pressure. See "Contacting Admissions: Mistakes, Interviews, Deferrals, Waitlists, and LOCIs" chapter for more.

16. Your early application decision will arrive online in your college portal on or around December 1 – 15th. If you're accepted and you filed your FAFSA and CSS Profile on time, there will be a tab or link to click on that will display your financial aid offer. Print out the financial aid offer and put it in the corresponding manilla college folder that already contains a printout of your application. This is useful to have if the offer changes. When mail arrives from admitted colleges, store it in their corresponding folder. After these early decisions, you'll know whether you need to apply regular decision (RD). RD applications are generally due on or about January 1 which means there will only be about two weeks to apply regular decision after receiving your early decisions. Check the regular decision application due date for each college because it can vary by a few days. The Common Application has a calendar on its dashboard that tells you when your applications are due. Order transcripts and ACT/SAT scores and make sure they arrive. Write additional essays. Submit RD applications a few days before they're due on or around January 1st.

17. If you were deferred in the early application round, write a Letter of Continued Interest (LOCI) to your admission officer. See "Contacting Admissions: Mistakes, Interviews, Deferrals, Waitlists, and LOCIs" chapter for more. Since deferred applications are considered alongside regular decision applications, you want your second LOCI to arrive in your application file for admission officer review in early to mid-January.

18. After you submit your RD applications, you typically won't get a decision until the end of March. If during the wait you receive good news about your GPA, honors, awards, or other accomplishments, then send an email to your admission officers updating them. They'll add the update to your application file for consideration. Some college applicant portals allow you to upload the letter in PDF form directly into your application file; do so but also email your admission officer a copy so that they know your file has changed.

19. Once your RD decisions arrive at the end of March, if it's good news then you're done. If you're waitlisted at a college that you want to attend, then you may want to email them a "Letter of Continued Interest" (LOCI). Consider including a new letter of recommendation. One from a teacher or someone in the community. See "Contacting Admissions: Mistakes, Interviews, Deferrals, Waitlists, and LOCIs" chapter for more. If you were accepted RD, then you'll typically have until May 1 to accept the offer of admission. There will not be any admission offers made from the waitlist until after May 1st because colleges want to wait until after their regular decision admits have decided whether or not to attend.

20. Ask your guidance counselor for local scholarship links and applications in late December/early January. Local scholarship applications are typically due in February and March. Work with your guidance counselor to submit these scholarship applications. You'll receive decisions before or at graduation.

Chapter Five

How to Maintain a High GPA

"This is wrong." Eiche shook his transcript at me in the kitchen. "It says I got a 95 in Spanish III instead of a 96. I've calculated it, and I should have a 96." I took the transcript from him to see for myself. "Did you email Ms. Noriega?" I asked. "Yes, and she agrees with my calculations. We're wondering if there's something wrong with PowerSchool?"

Your high school transcript is one of the most important factors college admissions considers because it predicts college success.

How high does my GPA need to be?

Do a mix of A and B grades mean you won't be admitted to an ivy level university? Top colleges admit students in and around the top 1-3% of their graduating class; however, during holistic review other factors are considered that could have negatively impacted your ability to achieve like difficulty of courses or personal circumstances. For example, maybe you challenged yourself with a particularly tough academic schedule? Or, maybe you needed to watch your siblings or help grandparents after school? Or, perhaps you worked long hours at a part-time job to help your family make ends meet? Colleges take such extenuating circumstances into account if you tell them about it in your application. You can do so in the additional information section or essays. So, the long answer is that if you have a mix of A and B grades, then you still have a chance; however, most students who get into top universities like the Ivies, Stanford, Duke, MIT, and the like have A grades in all their classes or nearly so. They've also taken the most challenging courses their high school offers. Getting into a top college is years of hard work.

Tips to help you maintain a high GPA.

1. **Study the syllabus.**

   For each class, make sure you have a syllabus detailing how much homework, test scores, and other assignments are worth. For example, Homework 10%, Quizzes 30%, Final Exam or Paper 40%, Class Participation 20%. This will help you determine which assignment, quiz, and test scores matter most, and you'll know where to concentrate your efforts. Additionally, when issues arise about your final grade, the syllabus is essential for figuring out whether your grade is correct.

2. **Calculate your own GPA.**

   Along with studying the syllabus, this is the most important tip to maintain high grades: always calculate your GPA yourself. Even if your grade is good, recalculate it. My kids were relentless about this. They would calculate their GPA in all their classes multiple times a semester. Often, they'd discover that a teacher failed to weight an assignment or quiz in accordance with the syllabus. Or, they'd find missing make-up grades or extra-credit grades. My kids sometimes even discovered inaccuracies with the high school's computer grading program. Teachers and guidance counselors are reasonable people. If you calmly and politely show them a mistake, then they will correct it.

   One of the most infamous examples of this in our family was when Eiche completed Spanish III and received a 95. According to his calculations, he should have received a 96. He and his teacher Ms. Noriega reviewed the grades in PowerSchool (his high school's grading program) and discovered a weird glitch. The semester was divided in half into quarters (two quarters equaled one semester), and PowerSchool computed quarter grades to send to families halfway through the semester. There had been an extra credit assignment completed in the first quarter that was missing, so Ms. Noriega added it to the first quarter after first quarter grades had closed. When the final grade came out for the course after the second quarter, Eiche and Ms. Noriega discovered that PowerSchool was not calculating the extra credit assignment into his final grade for the semester. They theorized it was because the extra credit grade had been entered after the first quarter ended, and although PowerSchool let them enter an additional grade it did not include it when calculating the final grade for the semester. Ms. Noriega added the grade to the second quarter instead and that solved the problem.

If Eiche had not been diligent about checking his GPA, then he would've received a 95 for Spanish III instead of a 96. This might seem trivial, but a 95 corresponded to a 3.75 and a 96 to a 4.0 course GPA. A big deal if you're trying to maintain a 4.0 cumulative GPA.

3. **Go beyond the minimum to earn a 4.0 in each class.**

When my older two kids were in high school, an A (4.0) was a 96 or above. By the time Lauren got there, an A (4.0) was 90 or above. This tempted her to get a 90 in each class because it translated to a 4.0 GPA—why work harder for a grade above a 90 when there's no change to your GPA? But she decided it would be better to do what her brothers did and aim for a 96 or above in all classes. Why? Since top colleges look for students who go beyond the required high school curriculum, Lauren surmised that they may also be looking for students who go beyond the bare minimum for a 4.0.

Additionally, the new grading scale presented a challenge for Lauren that her brothers didn't face. It was now harder to convince teachers to give extra credit or a grade higher than a 90. "You already have an A, so why do you want extra credit?" or "You already have an A so getting over a 90 won't make a difference in your GPA." Lauren understood their point of view; however, she knew it mattered for her college applications. Explaining that to them usually changed their minds.

4. **Don't give up if teachers resist changing grades because they think it doesn't matter.**

   My kids would discuss a grading error with a teacher in terms of hard work and fairness. For instance, "I've worked hard in this class, and I think I deserve the grade that I earned." When politely explained in terms of hard work and fairness, we found that teachers would correct an error—no matter how small.

5. **Fix low grades immediately**.

   Even the most brilliant kid stumbles and gets the occasional B or less. Address those stumbles when they happen. Don't wait until the end of the semester when teachers are busy, cranky, and likely to argue it's too late to change your grade. Below an A on an exam or homework? Ask for a do-over or extra credit work to make it up. If they don't accept extra credit work, then wait a week and approach them again. We found that some teachers would change their minds and agree even when the syllabus stated otherwise. If you're sick and miss in-class notes or quiz, then ask for a copy of the teaching notes and/or immediately schedule a make-up quiz. My kids found that teachers didn't mind sharing their lecture notes and would sometimes even provide them online. It's also a good idea to get to know your teachers by asking questions and contributing during and after class. Teachers are a lot more helpful with grades once they know a kid is a nice person as well as a serious student. And, getting to know teachers is a big plus when it comes time to ask for recommendations for college applications.

6. **Find study time wherever you can.**
   Try to get as much homework done during the school day as possible. My kids were involved in lots of extracurricular activities that limited their study time after school. They found time to study by diligently using free time during lunch, on a bus or car ride, and after school while waiting for activities to start. There were a few times junior and senior

years when my kids were up quite late working on school work. It's just the way it is. Getting into a top university is hard work. Besides, working the occasional late night in high school will help prepare you for college where late nights are often required.

7. **Register for a class each semester that provides flexibility for extra study time.**

For example, it's a good idea to register for at least one online course that can be used for study time at school when necessary. You can do the online class later at home. Also, if you schedule dual enrollment classes that take you off campus, you may discover extra time to do homework or study for a test before you return to your high school.

Chapter Six
SAT, ACT, SAT II and Test Optional

"A 29 composite on the ACT is pretty good for a sophomore." I sought to reassure her, but Lauren wasn't having it. "My English score is a 25. No one in our family has ever gotten a score that low." I offered help. "I'll search Reddit for an ACT English review book, and then we could do it together over the summer. Let's try to outscore each other on practice tests," I suggested. "That sounds fun," Lauren agreed. That summer we used a review book to relearn grammar and faced off on ACT exercises and practice tests. We had a rule that if one of us got a question wrong, then the person who got it right had to explain why to the person who got it wrong. If we both got it wrong, then we'd look up the answer together. We were super competitive, and our scores were quite close. The winner good naturedly taunted the loser. It was so much fun. Lauren retook the ACT (as a junior) six months after the first one and raised her English score to a 35—10 points! Her composite score was a 33. She was done taking the ACT.

Why do top colleges require these tests?

Colleges require them because they provide a baseline of academic aptitude. These schools receive 30,000 - 60,000 applications per year each with high school transcripts that use different grading scales. Colleges use these standardized tests to objectively assess academic ability.

Should I take the SAT or the ACT?

Try both SAT and ACT questions to see which you like best. My kids did better on the ACT. For many the opposite is true—the SAT is a better fit. And there are kids who take both exams because they do well on both.

We discovered the ACT out of necessity. After studying all summer for the SAT, Eiche received low scores. He was surprised. I was concerned. He'd studied quite hard over the summer using old exams under timed conditions. I honestly didn't think more studying would make a difference. I searched the Web for advice and discovered the ACT. I'd never heard of it before. When I was in high school in Massachusetts during the late 70s and early 80s, the only standardized test offered or even discussed was the SAT. As a sophomore, Eiche tried some of the ACT questions online and then without further practice sat for an actual exam a few weeks later. He received a 30 composite score. We realized that getting a 30 without prep meant it was the exam for him. He studied using old exams under timed conditions during the summer between sophomore and junior years and received a 34 composite.

When should I take the ACT or SAT?

If possible, you should be done taking these exams by the end of junior year because you'll need the summer between junior and senior years for writing college essays and applications. To get scores you're happy with by junior year, you'll need to prep over two summers.

- **Prep for the ACT or SAT during the summer between freshman and sophomore years.** Take the exam in September or October sophomore year while your prep is fresh. Taking the exam sophomore year will give you practice handling exam stress, and from the results you'll learn where to concentrate your prep for the junior year exam. Why are the PSAT and PreACT sophomore year not good enough practice? Because they're less grueling than the actual SAT or ACT.
- **Prep again the summer between sophomore and junior years.** Take the exam in September or October junior year while your prep is fresh. If you're unhappy with your score, study on weekends and take it again junior year.

How should I study for the SAT or ACT?

The SAT and ACT are unlike IQ tests in that one can significantly raise their score by studying. We couldn't afford a tutor or an online prep course, so my kids studied themselves using old exams under timed conditions.

- **Use the official SAT or ACT prep guides sold by them which contain complete exams.** If you run out of exams, there are more online available from ACT and SAT. Also, there are older editions of the official SAT and ACT prep guides on eBay that contain exams. These exams make fine practice because the concepts tested remain the same; however, some of the question types have changed over the years. Consider also other unofficial prep books containing exams which can be good practice. Keep in mind that they aren't actual exams and may be easier or harder. My kids liked Barron's test prep books because they found the exams harder than actual ACT exams.
- **Spend fifteen hours or so per week on test prep.** Pick a 4-5 hour block of time three times a week to study. Make a schedule like every M, W, F and stick to it over the summer. My kids, for example, would take two sections of an exam under timed conditions and then review their incorrect answers each study session.
- **Do your exam taking and studying in a place with no distractions.** My kids studied in the dining room and used a timer on the nearby kitchen microwave. They didn't use their cell phone because it's a distraction.
- **Take the sections in the order they appear on the exam because you want your brain to get used to thinking about those subjects in that order.** This is important for the ACT because the sections always appear in the same order on the exam.
- **Correct the sections and then, most importantly, review the answers you got wrong until you understand why.** You will not improve your score unless you review your mistakes and understand why you got each question wrong.

This kind of review takes time and is why you'll need a couple of hours each study session.
- **After a while you'll see patterns of certain question types that you're getting wrong.** Concentrate your studying on getting better at those question types.
- **If you need help in a subject area, like science, math, English, reading sections, search Reddit or other college forums for suggestions about what study guides to get to improve your scores.** If used diligently, a good study guide can turn your weakest section into your strongest. That's what happened to Lauren. She used a study guide that was widely recommended on Reddit and increased her English score from a 25 to a 35.
- **At the end of the summer, take a real SAT or ACT full-length exam at home under timed conditions.** My kids liked to do this to see how they would do on a full-length exam after a summer of prep.

How many times should I take the ACT or SAT?

College admissions doesn't want applicants taking the ACT or SAT more than three times. They'd rather you spend time pursuing your interests and working on your applications.

Should I retake if my score is a little below my dream college's average score?

During holistic review, admission officers consider factors other than grades and standardized test scores. This means that if you have a lower-than-average ACT or SAT score for their university, admissions will consider other factors in your application that could account for that. So, if your score is one or two points lower than the average for your dream college, you may want to consider applying without retesting.

In our family, for example, Max, the paper spaceship maker, took the ACT twice junior year and got a 32 composite both times. He had a 34 in the math section and a 33 in the science section. He planned to apply early decision (ED) to Duke for mechanical and aerospace engineering. At that time in 2016, the average ACT composite score at Duke's Pratt School of Engineering was a 33. Max asked my advice about whether he should take the ACT again to try for a 33. I advised against it. His scores in the ACT math and science sections were right on for Pratt, and I thought Duke admissions would consider his circumstances—small high school with limited resources—in holistic review. Also, I firmly believed that an extra point on a standardized test wasn't going to make or break his application, and that his time would be better spent writing excellent essays. "If they like you and want to admit you, then they will." I told him. "A point or two on a standardized test isn't going to stop them." Max didn't retake the ACT and was admitted ED to Duke engineering with a 32 composite score. It's worth repeating: If they like you and want to admit you, then they will. Admissions won't sweat the small stuff (like a point or two on a standardized test) if they want to admit you. Remember that as you reach for the stars with your applications.

What is superscoring?

Superscoring means admissions will consider only your highest section scores from multiple ACT or SAT exams. For the ACT, some colleges that superscore will even recalculate your composite score using your highest scoring sections. Research the colleges to which you're applying to see whether they superscore and, if so, what method. In September 2020, the ACT began offering students the option to send their own superscore reports to colleges if they'd taken the exam more than once. When Max applied to Duke in 2016, Duke admissions policy at that time was not to superscore the composite score; if they had, then he would've felt more secure about not retesting because his ACT composite superscore would've been considered a 33 rather than a 32.

More exam tips

- **If you qualify for an ACT or SAT fee waiver**, get that from your guidance counselor and use it to register for the exam.
- **Two or three weekends before the exam, take a full-length practice exam at home** starting at 8 am which is the start time of the actual exam. This will get you used to getting up at 8 am on a weekend and thinking hard early on a Saturday morning. It will also get you back in the groove of taking the exam which you might have slipped out of since the summer.
- **The night before the exam, pack a bag of what you'll need** including a healthy snack for the break, ticket, a watch (to pace yourself in case there's no clock), a mask (Covid-19), calculator (check testing rules for acceptable model), and identification. Then, go to bed early and get good quality sleep.
- **On test day, eat a healthy breakfast and dress in layers to adjust for warm or cold conditions.**

Should I take SAT II subject tests?

Most colleges no longer require them. Check admission websites of the colleges to which you're applying. Even so, some applicants look to enhance their applications by taking and submitting them anyway. In my opinion, additional standardized testing is not a meaningful way to enhance your application.

Covid-19 considerations

Before the Covid-19 pandemic, top colleges required either ACT or SAT scores. Due to a lack of safe testing locations, top colleges have gone "test optional." Test optional means that scores are not required but if you submit them, then they will be considered. Notice that top colleges could have removed ACT/SAT scores entirely from their admission process—but didn't. Since they'll still be considering scores, you should submit good scores if you have them. If you don't and can take an ACT or SAT safely, study and do so.

- **Consider including PSAT or PreACT scores in your application.** As the ACT/SAT optional decision demonstrates, the Covid-19 crisis has made admission offices more flexible about their rules. Given this flexibility, if you're unable to schedule a test or test safely, consider including PSAT or PreACT scores in your application if they predict a good range. According to the ACT testing service, PreACT scores "predict your future performance ranges when taking the full ACT in a year's time assuming typical achievement growth." So, reporting your PreACT or PSAT scores could help admissions confirm your academic aptitude. List your scores in the additional information section of your application along with an explanation that these are PSAT or PreACT scores that predict future SAT or ACT performance. Or, ask your guidance counselor to include the scores as part of their recommendation. Do not enter the scores in the testing section of the Common Application (or Coalition Application) because they're not actual SAT or ACT scores.
- **Your transcript, extracurriculars, and essays will be more important than ever.** Since Covid-19 disrupted transcripts (online classes and pass/fail grading) and standardized testing, college admissions will have less information to go on. Therefore, admission officers will be relying on other parts of your application more than ever. You'll need to focus even harder on your honors, activities, recommendations, and essays to make them the best they can be in content and presentation.

Chapter Seven

A Spiky Ball
Extracurricular Activities

It was parents' weekend 2016 at Duke University, and Max was a proud freshman showing us his dorm, Pegram. Next to a ping pong table in the common room, I noticed a white board containing a list of names. "What's this?" I asked. "Oh, that's the results of our tournament," Max replied. "See here. I'm seventh place." Perplexed, Lauren pointed to first place. "What's this? 'Max's Ego' is number 1?" We burst out laughing. Max has always had abundant self-confidence, and I was impressed that his Duke classmates figured that out so quickly. As we walked out of Pegram and onto the quad, Max remarked, "Everyone here does a lot of things well. It's a little intimidating. Remember when I was doing activities in high school, and we talked about how important it was to have a spike? Well, I think it's more like you need to be a spiky ball—well rounded with a spike or two."

What kind of extracurricular activities do top colleges look for?

What you love to do. Authenticity. It could be academic clubs, sports, job, internship, student government, community service, hobbies, or a mix. How you spend your free time is one of the ways colleges get to know you through your application.

Find a spike.

Elite universities look for students who've done something that makes them stick out from the crowd. This is commonly known in college admission forums as your "spike." You'll need at least one such activity. Why? Well, imagine what it's like being an admission officer at a top college reading hundreds of applications. The most common activities like band, sports, drama, art, and student government are seen over and over again. With grades, standardized test scores, and activities so similar among the applicants it's the unusual applications that stick out. There are two kinds of spikes: specialist and unique activity.

1. **Specialist**

    Admission deans and officers say they're looking for "specialists," and with so many well-rounded kids applying that's understandable. A specialist is someone who has taken a deep and devoted interest to new heights. In other words, they're looking for students who sink their teeth into something—activity, project, hobby, or other pursuit—and run with it. You don't have to be a world-ranked chess player, national spelling bee champ, Olympic qualifying athlete, though these qualify. You can simply be someone who spent hundreds of hours engrossed in something they love. As mentioned earlier, for example, Max was fascinated with origami in middle and high school. Origami itself is not all that unusual, but it's what happened overtime with this hobby that caught the attention of Duke admissions. By the time he got to high school, he developed an intense interest in and love for spacecraft. His shelves were full of paper models. When he applied early decision to Duke for mechanical/aerospace engineering, he submitted an art portfolio containing photos of his origami and spaceships. After he was admitted, Max received a congratulatory postcard from his Duke admission officer. She noted that what stuck out to her in his application was his "passion for spacecraft design."

2. **Unique Activity**

    A unique activity is one that isn't typically found on college applications. One of Lauren's spikes, for example, was that she was a goat wrangler. She volunteered with local farmers for a couple of days in spring and fall to wrangle goats for shearing and vaccination. As an environmentalist, this activity was consistent with her narrative. She was admitted regular decision to Davidson, Duke, and Princeton. She received a congratulatory postcard from her Davidson admission officer listing three things he liked about her application and "goat wrangling" was among them. Why did Davidson like this? Probably for the same reason Duke and Princeton did—because it was something unique, consistent with her narrative, and showed a commitment to help her community. I also think it brought a particular local flavor or geographic diversity to campus. How many kids at Princeton do you think are goat wranglers?

Be a spiky ball.

These types of activities come from the heart. Max loved making origami and spacecraft models. He graduated from Duke in 2020 and still makes them. The best way to find a spike is to find something that excites you so much that you spend hours and hours on it—or find something unique to do, or both. In addition to goat wrangling, Lauren is an avid watercolor artist. Senior year, her high school's "Night of the Arts" community showcase featured a climate change inspired collection of watercolor paintings that she'd been working on since junior year.

It's important to realize, however, that we're talking about one or two activities in which you specialize and/or do something unusual. You'll have plenty of ordinary activities too. Max played varsity and competitive soccer, earned a second degree blackbelt in taekwondo, played flute, and volunteered at a community thrift store. Most kids who are bright and curious enjoy doing lots of things well. By all means, keep the activities you enjoy. And when you list them on your college applications, you'll be competing against thousands of others who are similarly well rounded. Since well roundedness tends to blend in with the other applicants, the goal with your activities is to be well rounded with a spike or spikes: a spiky ball.

Do I need community service?

The answer is authenticity. Colleges don't care what you spend your time on as long as it's meaningful to you. Community service was not a focus for my kids. Even so, I encouraged a few hours per year to support the community. To find the time in their already packed schedules, they added a community service component to at least one activity. Lauren, for instance, played flute at church. She and another church flautist performed spring concerts at local elder care communities. Lauren also learned to program in Java at a summer camp. The following year, she was invited to tutor middle school students in Java and math at a middle school afterschool program. The point is that she was already spending time playing flute and programming in Java; she just expanded those activities to include community service.

Is there a point system for regional, state, national, and international recognition?

College admission counseling websites and YouTube videos discuss elite colleges using a point system to evaluate applications and contend that to get maximum points in the honors and activities sections an applicant must have national or international recognition.

How can you get this kind of recognition? If you're not an Olympic qualified athlete or national spelling bee winner or the like then you're going to have to get creative. Max was a varsity soccer goalie and won two regional goalie of the year awards. I was doing the typical mom thing of geeking out over his recent game stats on MaxPreps when I discovered that he was number one in saves in North Carolina and number two in the nation. He included that information in his college application's activities section. Lauren competed in national taekwondo tournaments and placed in the top four a couple of times. She was never number one, but you don't have to be the best; rather, any type of national recognition will do.

What could you do? Consider entering a national math, science, or writing competition, or pick an activity that gives you the chance to compete at the state and national level. Maybe publish scientific research, short stories, poetry, or a novel? Start a website that gets a lot of visits from around the world. Or, start a nonprofit that gets international visits to its website. Google for more ideas. And watch for recognition out of the blue. Lauren participated in a grant-funded, programming camp where kids learned Java to program Minecraft modules. They emailed her school to tell them that her module was the best they'd seen worldwide in three years. We printed out the email and evaluation form and saved it in a drawer where we kept her high school honors and awards. When it was time to fill out college applications it was there waiting for her.

How to make time for activities?

My kids struggled during high school to balance homework and activities. Here's what worked for them.

- **Time activities so they are spread out throughout the year.** My kids did activities scattered over the school year, summer months, spring break, and weekends. Also, they declined participation in activities that were so common that colleges barely notice them on applications like National Honors Society, FFA, DECA. If you love these activities then continue to do them. Authenticity. Just be aware that elite college admissions take little notice.
- **Consider limiting your activities to those that fit your narrative and dropping those that don't.** Over time as you try different activities and courses, you'll develop interests in certain things. Maybe you'll discover a strong passion for the environment? And an interest in theatre arts? If so, those will likely be things you'll talk about in your college essays. Part of your narrative (story) could be "the basketball playing environmentalist who loves designing sets for school plays." You'll be able to craft your application with your story in mind. See chapter "Create a Narrative to Focus Your Application" for more.
- **Pick activities that take little time but pack a powerful punch.** Part of Lauren's narrative, for example, was being an environmentalist. She was a goat wrangler helping local farmers with sheering and vaccinations. This activity

required only one weekend in the spring and fall. In sophomore year, she added a summer activity of a three-day environmental camp held by her county's soil and water district to clean streams and repair hiking trails. Not a lot of time devoted to these activities, but they were impactful because they reinforced her narrative. The summer between her sophomore and junior year she became a vegetarian and started cooking her own meals. We didn't realize that her vegetarianism reinforced her narrative until she started brainstorming for essays. See how reinforcing your narrative begins to naturally and spontaneously come together by simply following your heart? Authenticity.

What if difficult family or economic circumstances prevent activities?

What if you're in a situation where you cannot devote time to extracurricular activities? Sometimes there are difficult family or economic circumstances beyond your control. That happened to me. I was ten when my dad suddenly died. My mom started working full-time. I had to quit the soccer team to take care of my sister after school. To help out financially, when I turned sixteen, I got a job counting checks and stuffing statements into envelopes at a local bank. I took the bus to work every day after school and didn't get home until 7:00 pm. Then I'd eat dinner, study, and go to bed.

If you have a similar story, don't despair. Colleges want to know about jobs needed to support yourself, or siblings, grandparents you've cared for or other family obligations. These are extracurricular activities as impressive and important as being captain of the football team or club president. When you fill out your college applications describe whatever job or family responsibilities you've had in the activities section, the additional information section, or in essays.

Special admission programs are a spike.

Programs like QuestBridge and Leadership Enterprise for a Diverse America (LEDA) are free and offer an alternative college application process for low- and moderate-income high school students. Talk to your guidance counselor and search the Web to learn more. Top colleges partner with these organizations to increase numbers of low- and moderate-income students on campus. Students apply to be QuestBridge or LEDA scholars during their junior year of high school. Applications from these programs stick out in the college admission process because QuestBridge and LEDA scholars are financially and academically vetted by their respective programs. Students get their college admission decision early and receive full or substantial scholarships. Visit program websites to apply. We didn't learn about these programs until Lauren was a senior in high school. If we'd known about them, then my kids probably would've applied for QuestBridge.

Covid-19 considerations

Colleges understand that the pandemic makes many activities impossible for now. List what you did pre-Covid in the activities section of your application and explain any abrupt stop or change in the additional information section. Despite Covid circumstances, the problem of how to make yourself a spiky ball remains. Think about what you're currently involved in. Is there a way to help your activity and its community continue despite the pandemic? Being a problem solver who builds bridges during this difficult time could be a spike. For now, long distance travel is problematic. You'll have to get creative and find new ways to help you stick out whether online, at home, or in small groups in your community.

Chapter Eight

You Can Afford It
Need Blind vs. Meet Full Need Colleges

"Mom, I got some bad news from Clemson. Take a look at this email from financial aid." Eiche set his open laptop down on our kitchen counter. My eyes boggled. The combination of scholarships, federal grants, and loans left a balance of about $25,000 for our family to pay. "I don't understand this," I said. "According to the FAFSA our expected family contribution is zero. How can they expect us to pay $25,000?"

When I coached my first teenager through the college admissions process, I thought "need blind" admission meant "meet full need"; boy, was I wrong. Not understanding the difference between these terms can be a financial disaster. It almost was for us.

"Need blind" means that a college's admission office will consider applications without knowing whether or not the applicant and their family can pay the cost of attendance. "Meet full need" means that a college's financial aid office will meet 100% of a student's financial need with a combination of loans and grants once a student is admitted.

You can afford meet full need colleges. Don't let sticker shock stop you from applying.

As we all know, college is expensive. Googling reveals the cost of attendance (tuition + room, board) at an Ivy League university for 2019-2020 averaged about $70,000. When people see this high cost, they give up. "Why apply if I can't afford to go?" What they don't understand, however, is that the ivies and other top colleges like Stanford, Davidson, Rice, Duke, MIT, Vanderbilt, to name a few, are meet full need. In other words, if you have financial need and are accepted, then you won't be paying sticker price. Meet full need schools will make sure you can afford to go by providing a financial aid package of grants and loans. And, moreover, these schools typically limit student loans to 5-7 thousand per year. Some even meet your financial need loan free! Yes, you can afford it if you apply to and are accepted at meet full need schools. Lauren, for example, was offered a financial aid package from a top, meet full need private university that made her cost of attendance there less than in-state tuition, room and board at a state university.

Don't waste time applying to colleges that are not meet full need if you cannot afford it.

While picking colleges to apply to, Eiche's priorities were to find a school within a six-hour drive that offered an undergraduate degree in chemical engineering. He also wanted a suburban campus, great food, and a good academic reputation. Using that criteria, he applied to seven schools, and when decisions were released his financial aid packages were a surprise and not in a good way. He applied to need-blind schools, and we mistakenly thought this meant that those schools would meet all his financial need with loans and grants. He was admitted to Clemson University, University of Kentucky, University of South Carolina, Penn State University, North Carolina State University, University of Virginia, and Virginia Tech.

I was dismayed by the financial aid offers. We were a low-income family with an expected family contribution (EFC) calculated by the FAFSA as zero, yet almost all of the schools offered scholarships, federal grants, and loans that left a bill of about $20,000 or more for us to pay. Our family could not afford that. We then realized that Eiche wasted time applying to colleges we couldn't afford. Luckily, one of the schools he applied to was "meet full need" and another had a low-income program for in-state students. The University of Virginia was "meet full need" and offered Eiche grants and loans making it possible for him to attend. North Carolina State University was not a "meet full need" school but had a program for low-income, in-state students called "Pack Promise" which would meet all of Eiche's financial need. We were lucky. We nearly ended up without a college for Eiche that our family could afford.

After that near disaster, I made sure that my other kids only applied to meet-full-need colleges. If you're low or middle income, search the Web for a list of "meet full need" schools. There are about 90 of them including the Ivies.

If a college is need blind, then how do they determine economic diversity?

There are a couple of ways. First, from your high school's report which provides admission officers an overview of your school (student demographics, number of students free/reduced lunch, number of advanced/AP classes, etc.). This report is submitted by your guidance counselor to each college to which you apply. Second, because applicants tell them either in their essays or other sections of their application. Since admission officers are looking for economic diversity, if you are from a low to moderate income and/or first-generation college family, tell them. Maybe you work after school to help your family make ends meet? Or, maybe you couldn't afford things others could? Details like these will come out quite naturally in your essays, and you should not feel ashamed to share. Authenticity.

Should you bother filling out the FAFSA, CSS Profile, and other financial aid applications if you think you don't qualify?

Yes. The reality is that elite colleges are so expensive that you'll likely get aid even if you think you won't. Use the net price calculator at college websites to determine your aid before you apply. It's anonymous and provides an accurate estimate of how much financial aid you'll receive. Midway through Lauren's high school years, our income increased, and we became a middle-income family. While she was applying to college, I wondered if it was still worth applying for financial aid. I used net price calculators and discovered that I could expect colleges to provide about half with grants and loans. Our experience is that net price calculators are accurate when compared to financial aid offers received after acceptance.

What about pursuing merit scholarships?

This subject could be a book of its own. The short answer is: yes, if you have time. There are national, state, corporate, organization, and local scholarships. Google to apply. Ask your guidance counselor for a list of local ones. Check the college websites of schools to which you're applying to see if they offer merit scholarships that you can pursue. My kids received primarily need based aid from meet-full-need colleges. In our experience, if you are accepted to meet-full-need schools, then you won't need merit scholarships.

Chapter Nine

Early vs. Regular Decision
Target a Specific College

"Is there one school you'd absolutely say yes to if you got in?" Without hesitation, Max replied, "Duke." He stared past our porch rail toward the lush, wooded hillside. "If I could get into Duke that would really be something," he nodded wistfully. "It sounds to me like you should apply early decision," I said. He turned to face me. "What's that?"

This is when strategy begins to play a big part in your college application process. And you've got to be strategic because it's incredibly difficult to get into top colleges. Long gone are the days when a student can expect to get in with a mix of A and B grades and a high standardized test score. Gone too are the days when a student can get straight A grades and a perfect score on the ACT or SAT and expect to get in. Yes, it's that competitive. There are simply too many academically near perfect and perfect students from around the world competing for too few spots. As previously mentioned, during a typical admission cycle each of these schools receives 30,000 to 60,000 applications. A search of the Web reveals that the class of 2025 acceptance rates (early and regular acceptance combined) for top US colleges were Brown 5.4%, Columbia 3.6%, Cornell 10.7%, Dartmouth 6.2%, Duke 5.8%, Harvard 3.4%, MIT 4.0%, Princeton 3.9%, Stanford 5.19%, UPenn 5.6%, Yale 4.62%. At each school, applying early increases your chance of admission. Early and regular decision acceptance rates for the class of 2025 are as follows:

Brown	Early 15.97%	Regular 4.03%
Columbia	Early 10.10%	Regular 3.00%*
Cornell	Early 24.04%	Regular 8.74% (2024)
Dartmouth	Early 21.25%	Regular 4.6%
Duke	Early 16.7%	Regular 4.3%
Harvard	Early 7.41%	Regular 2.58%
MIT	Early 4.8%	Regular 3.4%
Princeton	Early 15.8% (2024)	Regular 3.98%**
Stanford	Early unavailable	Regular 3.6% (2024)
UPenn	Early 15.0%	Regular 4.15%
Yale	Early 10.54%	Regular 3.42%

* Estimated
**Princeton canceled class of 2025 early admission due to covid pandemic.

You can apply to only one early program.

Clearly, there's an advantage to applying early, so why doesn't everyone? For a few reasons. First, not everyone can get their application ready in time to meet the early deadline. Second, some students want to wait until they have the benefit of a full semester of senior year grades to lift their grade point average before they apply. Third, the advantage may not be as good as it appears. Some colleges claim it isn't any easier to get in during the early round because they use the same standard of review as the regular decision round. And, they further contend that the competition may actually be greater in the early round because the most competitive students tend to apply early. A combination of these reasons may keep some students from applying early, but it's really the fourth and final reason that's the big one—according to the rules and restrictions of these early programs, students can apply to only one. That's right; you can use your early application advantage at only one of these elite colleges.

What's the difference between EA, ED, REA, and SCEA?

Top colleges call their early application programs by a lot of confusing names, but let's start with the two most common ones: Early Action (EA) and Early Decision (ED). EA schools like MIT, for example, allow you to apply early without making a commitment. In other words, early action is non-binding. You can apply early and if accepted still say no or shop around by waiting for your regular decision schools. Early Decision admission programs, on the other hand, are binding contracts. If you're admitted to a college under an early decision application then you must attend that college. Schools with an ED program include Brown, Columbia, Cornell, Dartmouth, Duke, and UPenn. According to their rules, if you apply to one of these schools ED, then you cannot apply early under another private college's early program. Harvard and Stanford call their early program Restrictive Early Action (REA) while Yale and Princeton call their early program Single Choice Early Action (SCEA). With REA and SCEA, you're free to accept or decline an offer of admission because you are not bound; however, you may not also apply to any other private college's early program.

The effect of these rules is that you can apply to only one elite college's early program. The only exceptions are that you may also apply EA to public colleges and to rolling admission programs at private colleges. If you apply ED to Duke, for example, you may also apply EA to the University of North Carolina Chapel Hill because UNC is a public university. Max and Lauren did that. Before you apply early to any top school carefully read and follow the rules of that college's early application program.

Will I lose the option to compare financial aid offers by applying ED? And, what if an ED school doesn't give me enough aid upon acceptance?

It's true that if you apply ED, you'll lose the ability to compare financial aid offers because you're bound and must attend if admitted. Use the net price calculator at the school's website prior to applying, so you'll have a good idea what financial aid to expect. Also, the Ivies and most near Ivies are "meet full need" schools meaning that they're committed to meet 100% of your family's financial need using a combination of grants and loans, so the risk of not being able to attend due to lack of aid is low. If you're admitted ED, then they'll make it affordable for you to attend. If you believe your financial aid offer does not meet your need, you can negotiate with the college's financial aid office. After trying to work it out, if you still believe the aid is insufficient, then the college will release you from the binding ED agreement leaving you free to apply elsewhere regular decision. My advice is if you feel strongly about shopping around and comparing offers from the regular decision round, then do not apply ED but rather choose an REA or SCEA college to apply to early and use the regular decision round to shop around.

Early admission strategy

Let's talk strategy. Since getting into any top college is extremely difficult, you'll want to pick some schools to apply to that are "safety schools"—colleges where you're likely to be admitted. These are schools that are below your stats (colleges with lower average ACT/SAT scores and GPA than yours) and/or are state schools where your in-state status gives you an advantage for admission. Apply using EA programs if these colleges have them and rules allow. With regular decision stats for all of the Ivy League level colleges being in the low single digits or near single digits in the case of Cornell, it's clearly a good idea to pick one ED, REA, or SCEA school to apply to early. Since you can only use this early application advantage for one college, you'll have to decide which school you would absolutely attend if accepted. This is even more important if you're applying under a binding program because you must attend if admitted.

Keep in mind that you don't have to apply early anywhere; rather, you can apply regular decision and keep all your options open. However, it's so difficult to get into elite colleges via regular decision that I strongly recommend applying EA to as many public colleges and rolling admission schools as possible and ED, REA, or SCEA to your one top choice. All of my kids applied early. Eiche didn't apply to a binding or restricted early program because he had no clear first choice school; however, he did apply early action to University of Virginia and NC State and was accepted. For Max, Duke was his dream school. He applied ED, but at the same time applied EA to the University of Virginia, NC State, and UNC. He was admitted ED to Duke and so withdrew his EA applications. Lauren also dreamed of Duke and walked the same path; however,

Duke deferred her ED application to their regular decision round. She ultimately ended up at Princeton, but that's a story for a later chapter.

Target a specific college?

Got a dream school? Applying to a restrictive early admission program? If so, you'll be targeting a specific school. Here are some tips.

- **Pay attention to the admission dean.** Find out who the admission dean is and then look for interviews. They love their job and are excited about their school. What they say will give you clues to what they tell their staff to look for in applications. You can google their name to find interviews, or search for college newspaper posts announcing early and regular decision admission and welcoming a new class. These articles typically feature a few statements by the admission dean regarding what they liked about or sought in the incoming class. Also, visit the admission department website to see if they describe what they're looking for in applicants. The information you learn can help you decide which of your characteristics to highlight in essays, as well as how to tailor your application narrative.
- **Learn what's unique about the college.** This is the same research you'll do for supplement essay "Why this college?". Research the college and find out what makes them special. Is it their world view? Do they have majors that other schools don't? Do they have a commitment to community service? Is their business school a big deal? Do they have a small but select engineering program? A unique internship opportunity program? Travel abroad options? Is there an overall philosophy or academic approach uniting that college's departments and community? Use this information for essays and to highlight honors and activities in your application.
- **Examine the college's Common Data Set (CDS).** The CDS is a report wherein you'll find all sorts of useful statistics like average financial aid award, academic

profile of the freshmen class, criteria for admission, faculty/student ratio, undergraduate class size, etc. Colleges produce their own CDS each year. Google the name of the college and the words "common data set" to find it.

Chapter Ten

College Admission Rules to Break

"Hey mom, Princeton requires four years of a foreign language, and I only have three!" Lauren shouted from her bedroom. It was mid-December. She had just been deferred early decision by Duke and was hard at work on her regular decision applications. "I've read online about students who applied to college without meeting all the requirements, and they still got in! Apply anyway!" I yelled back.

As you prepare to apply, you'll learn a lot about the colleges on your list. There will be campus visits and virtual tours. Just as essential are visits to each school's website to learn about their majors, programs, scholarships, and so forth. One of the most important online visits you should make is to the college's undergraduate office of admission. There, you'll learn about standardized tests and high school course requirements. This can present a problem. What if you took two years of a foreign language when three is required? Does this mean that you need to scramble to add a class to your senior schedule? Maybe it's too late to do that? Or, maybe you'd rather take something else you're more interested in? What if SAT II subject tests are recommended, and you haven't taken any?

Apply anyway. Don't let course, AP, or SAT II requirements or recommendations stop you. Over the years, I've seen numerous posts in various college forums from students who applied to colleges without all the required high school courses and/or SAT II tests scores and/or AP tests scores and they were admitted. Two of my kids were admitted to colleges without high school courses required by college websites. Remember, if they like you and want to admit you, then they will. Colleges won't sweat the small stuff during admission if they like you.

Remember too that elite colleges take into consideration what's available at your high school. If you're coming from a small school, then advanced classes may not be available. Also, if you've taken high school classes that fit your narrative, e.g., more math and science than required because you love it and want to be an engineer, then admissions will take that into account and likely overlook a missing high school class it requires because it's not essential to a future engineer's college curriculum. This is similarly true for students seeking to major in the humanities who may have less than the college's required high school math or science.

College admission rules to bend

As the ACT/SAT optional decision demonstrates, the Covid-19 crisis has made admission offices more flexible about their rules. Keep that in mind as you go through your application process in terms of what to submit in or with your application. Consider researching colleges that solicit unusual applications and try to incorporate some of those approaches into the standard applications that most elite colleges require. How about a college application video? Or pasting links to your website or YouTube project video in the additional information section? What about a creative portfolio submission via SlideRoom? These extras could tip an admission decision your way especially given the fact that academic transcripts and ACT/SAT scores have been negatively impacted by Covid-19.

If you have something extra that you believe is important to share but cannot figure out how, then discuss it with your guidance counselor. They may be able to include it in their recommendation. Or a teacher may be able to include it in theirs. Also, if the college you're applying to allows it, then consider an optional recommendation from someone in your community. In some ways, these are better than teacher recommendations because they focus on what you're like as a person rather than as a student. Take care, however, not to bombard admission officers with too many extras. Add one or two but no more. Rather than enhance your application, too many extras could have the opposite effect by causing admissions to question your judgment.

Chapter Eleven

Essay Brainstorming and Writing

When Lauren's early decision application was deferred by Duke to their regular decision round, she faced a crisis of confidence. She had only two weeks to apply regular decision to Ivy League schools but felt intimidated. "What could a simple, mountain girl like me from a small, rural high school possibly offer an Ivy League school?" Lauren wondered. "That's precisely what you do have to offer," I replied. "To have any hope of being admitted, you'll need to write essays emphasizing what's special about you and your community, and that you'll bring that to campus."

    The college application essay is personal. A personal essay is conversational, creative, and even inspirational. There isn't an introduction, thesis statement, or five paragraph format. You'll tell stories, use contractions, and employ any paragraph structure that makes sense. There will most likely be dialogue, and you'll be referring to yourself as "I". For the Common Application, you'll be writing a personal essay between 250 and 650 words. You'll have the freedom to express who you are; however, remember that your audience is college admission officers so keep it clean and polite. You want admissions to like you—not be offended by you. Also, don't include anything that would make them think you'd be a difficult roommate.
    There are seven Common Application writing prompts to choose from. Ignore them until you're done writing your essay. Any quality, personal essay will fit one or multiple prompts, and you can choose once you're done. Using the prompts now at the beginning of your writing process will intimidate, confuse, and maybe even mislead you thereby harming your process.

What are college admission officers looking for in a college essay?

College admissions use essays to learn who you are in your own voice. They're looking for personal growth. In other words, essays with lessons learned or insights gained. With thousands of students applying with near perfect grades and scores, it's the essays that often make the difference. That's a lot of pressure for kids to write under, and my advice is surprisingly simple—the best chance of standing out and impressing admission officers is to be yourself. Authenticity. When Lauren was deferred ED by Duke, she faced a crisis of confidence. She had two weeks to apply regular decision to Ivy League schools, but felt intimidated. "What could a simple, mountain girl like me from a small, rural high school possibly offer an Ivy League school?" she wondered. After a few soul-searching conversations, Lauren realized that it was precisely those attributes that would make her stick out. They were looking for authenticity. With fresh confidence, she wrote essays that told stories about creating art and helping her community. She was admitted to Princeton.

How do I make my essays stand out?

The best way to make your essay stand tall above the crowd is to tell an authentic and interesting story about yourself that engages the reader from the first line. Why a story? Because that's the best way to keep readers interested, stay memorable, and provide meaningful details about you. Consider Eiche's Common Application essay. He could have simply asserted, "I have grit and surmount obstacles" which is boring, forgettable, and provides little detail about him. Instead, he wrote a story about having paroxysmal vertigo and described how overcoming his parent's doubt about his illness was harder than overcoming the illness itself. Via analogy, he then discussed surmounting doubt to become a blackbelt and, later in high school, to win the science fair. From his story, admissions learned about him and drew their own conclusions regarding his character. He was admitted to the University of Virginia, among others.

Here's my five-step plan for writing the personal essay.
(Used by my kids.)

1. Step one: Brainstorm aka mining for gold (about 3 hours)

- Sit down with family or alone and make a list of any stories or memories about you that stand out. They could be anything ranging from when you were a child through high school age. They can be quirks, hobbies, or something you're known for in the family. Often simple things make the best essays.
- Is there anything you're known for around the community or at school? Stories from your job? Do you have stories about strong likes or dislikes or getting into and out of a jam?
    - How about things that are embarrassing, funny, scary, sad?
    - Conflicts or a juicy problem that you figured your way out of are particularly good.
    - How about sibling problems or an uplifting story about working together.
    - Conflicts at school or working well in a group?
    - Nicknames?
    - Family responsibilities?
    - Things you love to do or could not live without? Things you hate?

Make sure you have ten or more. You'll be using these ideas for your main personal essay and supplement essays so digging deep is well worth it. Think of it as mining for gold. On your laptop, create a folder called "college essays" and in that folder create a document for each essay topic. Paste or type the topic, memory, quirk, conflict, or whatever at the top of the document. When you save the document, name it for the memory or story. For example, if you were chased by bees, you'd name the file BEES. You're naming your bars of gold.

2. Step two: Freewriting (a few hours a day for a few days)

Open each of your saved files, type the word "Freewrite" at the top, and then beneath it write about the topic. Just let your thoughts and feelings flow without care about punctuation or grammar. My kids would write two stories a day for a week or two over the summer. For each story or topic, it's important that you describe:

- What happened?
- What you were thinking?
- How it made you feel?
- What did it smell, taste, sound, look like?
- The resolution, if any?
- How the resolution made you feel?
- What you learned from the experience (could be more than one thing)?

3. Step three: Making Connections (about 3 hours.)

To be done after you're done freewriting all your topics. Open each file and add a bunch of blank lines to the top, pushing down your freewrite to the bottom of the page but do not delete it. Above the word "Freewrite," type ten plus signs to create a horizontal line of plus signs like this ++++++++++ to separate your freewrite section from your connections section. In the blank space at the top of the page above the plus signs, type in the title "Connections" and then beneath the word "Connections" list all your personal qualities and characteristics that were evident in the story, positive or negative. Refer and reread your freewrite if necessary. For example:

- Were you diligent, hardworking but selfish?
- Were you inquisitive or inventive but overly eager?
- Were you brave, a risk-taker, or athletic but foolish?
- Intelligent, a leader, creative, kind, musical, autonomous, compassionate, insightful, funny, worked well in a group, artistic but disrespectful, clumsy, insensitive?

Think carefully about what the story says about you, and list every quality you can think of good and bad. Do this for each file. After you're done, take a piece of paper and write down:

(1) Which stories showed the most characteristics or traits?
(2) Which stories showed similar or same traits?
(3) Which stories showed unique characteristics not in other stories?

4. Step four: Pick your main essay story (an hour or less)

Use your piece of paper to consider all the stories you freewrote and pick the one that reveals the most about you or, in other words, shows the most character traits. This will be your main personal essay for the Common Application. For your essay to really sizzle and engage the reader you need to be excited about writing it. If you're not, then pick a story you love that reveals a few less characteristics. Just remember, the point is to tell a story that reveals a lot about you. If it reveals something negative that's okay as long as the negative thing is relatively minor and you apologized/made it right/learned from it. College admission officers aren't looking for perfect people; they're looking for people who aren't afraid to make mistakes and learn from them. Examine the connections you wrote down to other stories, and see if you can use those as mini stories to incorporate into your main personal essay via analogy and to further illustrate positive traits and what you learned.

5. Step five: Write your personal essay (a few hours a day for a couple of days. Maybe less depending on the quality of your freewriting.)

Edit the file that has the main story you selected.
- Type ten equal signs ========== above the word "Connections" that titles the character trait list you made. Use the enter key to give yourself lines of space to write by pushing down your "Connections" character trait list. Just to be clear, you now have a list of character traits below the equal signs, and you have your freewriting below the plus

signs. Just like a painter uses a palate of colorful paints to create their masterpiece, you'll use your freewrite and connections character traits to write your main essay for the Common Application in the blank space above the equal signs.

- Copy and paste sections from your freewrite into your main essay writing area above the equal signs to edit and expand as needed, but be careful not to delete any of the original freewriting. The freewriting you've done for each story are like bars of gold. Protect them. You'll need them for writing supplement essays and scholarship essays. And if you write something you don't like, you can always return to your freewriting for inspiration and to see the original way you expressed an idea.
- Scroll down and use your character trait list to consult after you're done writing your personal essay to see how well your writing communicates those traits. Revise your essay until you communicate your traits well. It's perfectly fine if your story focuses primarily on one trait and while telling that story other traits that you don't emphasize emerge. You want that to happen. You are multidimensional with lots of wonderful characteristics, and admission officers will note that as they read.
- As you write your essay, when you get to the point where you want to add a mini story to further illustrate traits and/or what you learned, open a new window with that mini story's freewriting file. Use it as reference for adding that to your main story. Be careful to copy and paste, do not cut. You want to keep the original freewriting for the mini story intact for future use.
- To prevent the annoyance of bouncing back and forth between windows, my kids would copy and paste sections of a mini story freewriting into the body of the main story essay and modify it there.

Techniques to make your personal essay stand out.

Numbers 1-6 are essential for a great personal essay. Pick and choose from numbers 7-12 to make your essay stand out even more.

1. **Show and explain.**

    "Show don't tell" is the essay advice shared most often by college essay experts, but it doesn't go far enough. As already discussed, you'll use stories to show a lot about you. Simply telling by listing your characteristics, e.g., hardworking, funny, athletic, is boring compared to an interesting, impactful story. But you need to do more than just show—you must also explain. Make sure your essay explains lesson(s) learned or insight(s) gained and how they impact you going forward. How much explanation to provide is up to you and is a matter of writing style. To see different approaches, here are examples from two of my kids' Common Application essays. I've edited them by replacing lines that tell the story with an ellipsis (…) to show only their explanations of lessons learned or insights gained.

    Example One: Eiche

    …

    Overcoming vertigo was daunting, but overcoming doubt proved a greater challenge.

    …

    I learned that surmounting doubt is part of every challenge.

    …

    As I grew, these lessons in confidence and tenacity helped me achieve in high school and beyond. Many times, I've had to convince doubting classmates of topics, methods, or roles in group projects. And to be fair, happily, they've convinced me too.

...

What about my parents? Did they learn their "vertigo lesson" to have faith in me?

...

My mom is coming around.

Example Two: Max

...

Although Lauren's intrusions annoyed me, they inspired her to make creations rivaling mine. As we grew, she became more like me than any little brother I could hope for. From art to athletics, Lauren shares my adventurous spirit. Wowing with imaginative origami and double back handsprings, she showed me that gender doesn't matter.

...

Ignoring the doubters and focusing on the position I love, I soon stood out on every rec, club, and varsity team rising from parents and players questioning why to admiration.

...

My steadfast hard work changed perception and motivated others.

...

Displaying compassion, inclusion, and fun brought our community together.

...

While growing up, these events taught me to follow my heart and stand my ground.

...

In Richard Bach's classic tale "Jonathan Livingston Seagull," Jonathan teaches heretical flying techniques in the midst of the flock. "Gray-feathered backs were turned upon Jonathan," but in a month "the first gull of the Flock crossed the line and asked to learn how to fly." Doing what you love can inspire others but only if boldly done. Courage is required particularly if what you want to do is unusual or unpopular. If I had not made jewelry, become a goalie, or adventured with Austin, those communities would not have changed. Similarly, the Big Ivy Community Thrift Store where I volunteer was started twenty years ago by a woman selling neighborhood donations out of her van. Where will my bold heart take me? Perhaps I'll become a mechanical, aerospace, biomedical, or computer engineer, artist, some combination, or something else. I can't wait to start.

2. **Hook your reader with your opening line.**

   The most effective way to do that is to start your story in the middle of the action. Here are my kids' hooks from their personal essays.

   The dizziness persists even in my sleep; repeatedly waking me and spawning odd dreams.

   The desk drawer jerks free flinging colorful paper stars, roses, lanterns, springs, and parrots.

   Spinning out of a half twist, I face-planted into my neighbor's trampoline net.

   Do they make you want to read more? A good hook should.

3. **Explain your future plans on-campus, after graduation, or both.**

   It can be just one or two lines, but you want to give admissions some indication of your future goals. You can do this in your main personal essay or in a supplement essay.

4. **Be human.**

   With perfect or near perfect scores and grades, consider an essay in which you're fallible. No one wants a know-it-all or perfect person as a roommate. Lauren started her essay with an embarrassing dilemma: she caught her braces in a trampoline net. Max's essay opening was about being annoyed by his pesky, younger sister poking around in his things.

5. **Admit you don't know something if you don't.**

   This relates to number four. You're not expected to know everything. As a teenager, you're just starting to figure things out. Don't be afraid to own that in your essays. Here's an example from Lauren's Common Application essay in which she wondered why her orthodontist wasn't angry that she'd busted her braces for a second time.

   He was far from mad—not even a warning! Was it because I obeyed the no candy rule? Or, was it because the office found it funny? Could it be that the first time he was having a bad day? All were probably true, but I kept thinking there was more to it. The puzzle found its way to my mind's back burner.

6. **Read your essays aloud.**

   Admission officers want personal essays that are conversational. Put yours to the test by reading it aloud. Does it sound like you? Does it sound like you're talking to someone over a cup of coffee? It should. I used to tell my kids that it should read as if you're sitting with the admission committee and speaking directly to them.

7. **Consider doing a montage.**

If you have different stories that illustrate a common trait, lesson learned, or both, then consider a montage—mini stories brought together to create a single essay. A montage can make an impact especially if you keep your reader guessing about how the mini stories relate until the end. Great for that Aha! moment. Be careful, however, not to confuse your reader. This happens when mini stories in a montage are too unrelated. Admission officers could then conclude that you don't know how to write coherently.

Max wrestled with this problem in his montage personal essay. His first three paragraphs were each a different mini story, and his fourth paragraph tied them all together. He knew it seemed disjointed but wasn't sure how to fix it. His English teacher stopped mid-way through reading the second paragraph to ask how it related to the first one. This convinced Max that he needed to find a solution because college admission officers would likely do the same. Max's solution was to link the first three paragraphs together stylistically by making the first sentence of each paragraph about opening a drawer and revealing its contents. He then titled his personal essay "Drawer Journeys." Problem solved. He was admitted early decision to Duke.

8. **Add some intellectual vitality.**

One of the things colleges look for in your essay is how well you think and reason. What do you reach for or consider as you draw your conclusions? I advised my kids to include a quotation from a favorite poem, song, book, or historical/political figure and explain how it impacted their views relating to their personal essay topic. In Max's essay, this consisted of two sentences in the last paragraph. In Lauren's essay, it was one sentence in the last paragraph. Make sure that you give full credit for any reference. Here's an example from the final paragraph of Max's Common Application personal essay from 2016.

In Richard Bach's classic tale "Jonathan Livingston Seagull," Jonathan teaches heretical flying techniques in the midst of the flock. "Gray-feathered backs were turned upon Jonathan," but in a month "the first gull of the Flock crossed the line and asked to learn how to fly." Doing what you love can inspire others but only if boldly done...

Max then discussed the three mini stories in his montage where he displayed courage to do something unpopular that helped others find the courage to do the same.

9. Add an ironic twist.

For example, the dizzy kid who becomes a second-degree black belt. Or, the vegetarian who flips burgers at the local fast-food joint.

10. Link your lesson learned or insight to popular culture or contemporaneous events in a way that's unexpected yet undeniably true.

See number 11 for an example.

11. Create an Aha! moment.

One of the things admission officers evaluate in your essays is how you think and reason. If you come to an unexpected conclusion that they never saw coming yet is undeniably true, you'll create an impactful Aha! moment they'll remember. In his personal essay, Max did a great job of this while also linking to current events of 2016 (at that time Bruce Jenner was transitioning and unisex bathrooms were big news). Here's how.

The desk drawer jerks free flinging colorful paper stars, roses, lanterns, springs, and parrots. I always wanted a little brother, but I got Lauren instead. "Pick them up when you're done," I sigh...Although Lauren's intrusions annoyed me, they inspired her to make creations rivaling mine. As we grew, she became more like me than any little brother I could hope for. From art to athletics, Lauren shares my adventurous spirit. Wowing with imaginative origami and double back handsprings, she showed me that gender doesn't matter.

12. Title your essay.

A good title increases interest by creating curiosity and providing readers a peek at your subject matter. When Max rewrote his montage essay so each paragraph started with the opening of a drawer, he also spent a few days thinking of titles. He liked "Drawer Journeys" because it gave the reader an immediate understanding of his essay's structure. He tested the title out on his brother and grandfather who hadn't yet read the essay. They said it sounded "interesting."

How to write supplement essays.

Supplement essays are challenging because they're typically small with a 150 – 250 word limit. You have to carefully pick each word and sentence. Warm up with your large Common Application essay then tackle the smaller supplements. Also, starting with your main personal essay will give you a better idea of what to write about in the supplement ones. You don't want to repeat what you wrote in the main essay. Admission officers hate repetition.

Despite their small size, in supplement essays you'll still need to tell a story with lesson learned or insight gained. If you write carefully and artfully, you can tell a nifty, little story that illuminates a lot about you. Let's discuss the two most common supplement essay types.

Supplement Essay Type #1: Tell us about an extracurricular activity.

Sometimes this prompt also includes "...that is meaningful to you." Whether or not it says so, you should always pick an extracurricular activity that is meaningful to you. Most applicants simply pick an activity from their activities section and write a bland recitation of what they did. This wastes a huge opportunity to tell admissions something new. It's also a good way to bore the heck out of them. Imagine the thousands of descriptions of swim team, football camp, track and field, marching band, and student government they've read?

Try to think of something that means a lot to you that isn't a typical extracurricular activity. It could be something you do for a friend or family member. Maybe it's time spent with a pet or a sibling? Perhaps use one of your mini essays from your essay brainstorming session? The more personal it is the better your answer will be because it will reveal more about you. As an example of how you can write about something completely unexpected, here's what Lauren wrote.

Prompt: Tell us about an extracurricular activity that is particularly meaningful to you. (Limit 150 words)

During the holidays, we didn't have a lot of money. My friends planned to exchange gifts that were store-bought items I couldn't match, so I searched the Web for ideas. Hand braided bracelets, patches, stickers for laptops, and tiny, painted pictures dominated the gift bags I gave to my friends.

I was nervous. Would they like what I made? My fears evaporated upon seeing Sydney's broad smile. She put on my bracelet and hugged me. Although I spent little to no money on handmade gifts, my friends seemed to appreciate them more. Was it because of the time I spent? Or, was it because they liked my art? Whatever the reason, I learned that the best gift is one you put your heart into. Whether choosing the right message for a patch or spending hours on a bracelet, it's the love put into the process that makes the result special.

See how these little essays can pack a powerful punch? Imagine how much this stuck out from the thousands about band camp, student government, internships, and soccer? Did the opening line make you want to read more? Was the essay grammatically correct? How many personal characteristics were illuminated? Was there a lesson learned? More than one?

Supplement Essay Type #2: Why do you want to attend our college?

This is a research prompt. You'll need to research the college's website, course catalogue, faculty, facilities, majors, job programs, abroad programs, clubs, etc. Given the word limit, you'll be able to meaningfully discuss two unique things. That's what to look for in your research. Your reasons why you want to attend must be specific. If your answer works for any other university, then you're not being specific enough. In your essay, you'll need to show how the university is a good fit for you, and how you're a good fit for them. That means weaving together what you're looking for and what you have to offer with opportunities at the university. As an example, consider Max's "Why Duke (Pratt Engineering)?" essay. (Limit 250 words)

> *I want to convert my passion for spacecraft design and construction into a practical engineering career. However, I'm also intrigued by the human body and creating medical devices. Duke provides the flexibility to explore possibilities where the faculty, facilities, and students are second to none. I could double major, minor, pursue a certificate, or create my own combination using Pratt's IDEAS program.*
>
> *Discoveries are made and marketed through a collaborative process. I want to create and market drones, medical devices, airplanes, and spacecraft. To that end, Pratt provides an engineering education uniquely focused on that process. For example, in Professor ___'s biomedical device innovation course students shadow doctors for inspiration, consult attorneys about intellectual property, and pitch ideas to venture capitalists. And*

in Bass Connections and DEV, interdisciplinary collaboration produces innovations ranging from groundbreaking research to an electric car prototype.

Did Max match his interests and goals to what the university offers? Was he specific enough? Could what he wrote apply to another university?

Reuse supplement essays to reduce your workload.

There are a lot of essays to write. To make the workload manageable, consider reusing essays by adapting them to similar prompts from other colleges. Essays about your favorite book or extracurricular activity, for example, are not college specific and are perfect to recycle. Sometimes prompts are similar enough that an essay can be adapted by changing the first couple of sentences or the ending. Just be sure to carefully edit. For instance, it would be bad for MIT admissions to read about your love for Duke.

Covid-19 considerations

In May 2020, the Common Application announced an optional, additional essay in the additional information section. Here's the essay prompt:

Community disruptions such as COVID-19 and natural disasters can have deep and long-lasting impacts. If you need it, this space is yours to describe those impacts. Colleges care about the effects on your health and well-being, safety, family circumstances, future plans, and education including access to reliable technology and quiet study spaces. (250 words)

- *Do you wish to share anything on this topic? Y/N*
- *Please use this space to describe how these events have impacted you.*

This question is optional, so you don't have to answer if you have nothing meaningful to share; however, if you've suffered any of the "deep and long-lasting impacts" listed from Covid-19 or other natural disaster, then write the essay. Just keep in mind that Covid-19 is a shared experience. If you write about hardships that are common, e.g., having to wear a mask, vacation was canceled, graduation/prom was canceled, you risk a "so what" response from admissions.

Chapter Twelve

Create a Narrative to Focus Your Application

After class, Max handed his college essay to his English teacher Mr. Rice to review. "Did you really do this?" He asked after finishing the first paragraph. "Do what?" Max replied. "Make space shuttles out of paper?" Mr. Rice clarified. Max nodded. "Wow," He muttered and resumed reading. At dinner that night, Max shared with us what happened adding, "Fingers crossed Duke says 'wow' too when they read it."

    The tens of thousands of applications received by top colleges are sorted geographically and assigned to admission officers by region. Regional officers are then responsible for shepherding their applications through the review process. They read them, make notations, and pass them on for a second evaluation by someone else on staff. Sometimes there's even a third or fourth read by staff. Applications are then presented to the admission committee by regional officers who advocate for their applicants. The committee votes to admit, defer, waitlist, or deny. With thousands of applications to review and present, admission officers don't have much time to read each application. Nor is there much time for committee discussion. Therefore, it's important for an applicant to submit an application that makes it easy for their regional admission officer to argue in favor of admission.

The one sentence pitch

Admission officers love an application that tells a memorable and thought-provoking story. And since they don't have a lot of time, they need to boil your application down to a simple pitch. Doing the same prior to writing your application will help you give your application focus and clarity thereby making it easier for admission officers to articulate your story and advocate for you. Your one sentence pitch will be the narrative or theme for your application. Now that you've brainstormed and written your personal essay, you know your strongest characteristics and best stories and are ready to create your application narrative. Here are the successful narratives my kids used for their applications.

> The dizzy kid who became a second degree blackbelt and dreams of being a chemical engineer.
>
> The nationally-ranked, soccer goalie who makes spaceships out of paper and dreams of being an aerospace engineer.
>
> The goat wrangler who caught her braces in a trampoline net and wants to combine art and technology.

Are they interesting enough to stick out from the crowd? Memorable? A good narrative should be. You want to make admission officers exclaim, "What about that dizzy kid who became a blackbelt? He's terrific!" Or, "I like that kid who made spaceships out of paper, what about him?" Or, "How about the girl who caught her braces in the trampoline net? She was great!"

Your narrative will help you throughout the college application process. My kids' goal for their applications was to convey their narrative clearly enough that admission officers could articulate it. A one sentence narrative will help you decide:

- Which activities and honors to list in your application and in what order.

- How to answer college and scholarship interview questions by quickly bringing to mind your most interesting stories and characteristics.
- What to add to your application to enhance it, e.g., portfolio, recommendations, and what to ask your guidance counselor, teachers, or members of the community to include in their recommendations.

How do I create my narrative?

It comes from your interests. By sophomore year of high school, and often earlier, you decide which activities to keep and ditch. As discussed in "A Spiky Ball" chapter, you kept activities you love (authenticity) with at least one specialist or unique activity as a spike. Your activities will help to make an interesting narrative or theme for your application.

To better understand the one sentence narrative, let's dissect Lauren's: the goat wrangler who caught her braces in a trampoline net and wants to combine art and technology. Each part of this narrative represents interests. "the goat wrangler" represents Lauren's interest in and commitment to the environment. It's also a spike. "...who caught her braces in a trampoline net" represents her interest in acrobatics and was the hook for her Common Application essay. "...and wants to combine art and technology" represents her interest in art and computer programming as well as her dreams and future plans.

Not everything you do will make it into your one sentence narrative. That's completely understandable given the number of interests and activities you have. Lauren, for instance, played flute in the community and competed in national taekwondo competitions. That isn't in her narrative. No problem. She still used these other interests to illustrate traits like grit and leadership in mini essays and in her activities section. Understanding that they were not a part of her narrative helped her to organize and focus her application sections, e.g., honors, activities, essays, to emphasize what was in her narrative.

Your application should be a story that makes sense.

In order to effectively tell your story, your application should be cohesive and make sense. Having a narrative will help you do that by tightening your focus. If you want to be an environmental science major in college, for example, does it make sense that none of the activities in your application are environmental? If you want to major in computer science, does it make sense that you didn't take comp sci classes in high school? If your extracurricular focus has been debate team and canvassing for political candidates, but you want to major in computer engineering, don't you think you should explain that disconnect in your application? The story your application tells about you should make sense given the facts in your application. If connections aren't apparent, then you need to explain how things connect via essays or the additional information section.

This was the case for Eiche who wanted to be a chemical engineer but had no extracurriculars and few high school courses in that direction. He wrote a supplement essay about carrying a periodic table pocket guide to read for fun, his life-long fascination with TV shows Nova and Modern Marvels, his attempt to audit high school chemistry in middle school, and his disappointment in high school with the lack of student interest in advanced science courses that led to course cancellations.

What if you want to apply as undecided or something different from what you did in high school?

Colleges accept large numbers of students who don't know what they want to major in. Own your undecidedness and make it part of your narrative. Be straightforward and say that you don't know or haven't decided. In your essays, discuss your interests and emphasize your open mindedness and eagerness to embrace any and all opportunities on and off campus. And if you want to do something completely different in college than you did in high school, use your high school activities to emphasize your character traits of determination, leadership, open mindedness, enthusiasm, service to the community, etc. and link these traits via essays to your college goals.

Chapter Thirteen

Make the Most of Each Application Section

"I'm sick of working on my honors and activities sections," Max complained. *"Take a break. Print them out and leave them on your desk, so you can review them to make changes over the next few weeks," I suggested.*

This chapter is about strategy: how to organize and write your application to stand out. The first step is to decide *what* to share, and the second is to decide *where* to share it. These are among the most important decisions you'll make in your application.

What to share?

Most high school students think of a college application as simply a form to fill out. Without a plan, they sit down at their laptop and fill in the blanks. This is a mistake. Your application is much more important to your future than a typical internet form. It is *you* for all intents and purposes during the college admission process. You need an effective plan to make sure each section sings in your voice with new and interesting information about you.

To be taken seriously as an applicant, your application must make sense by being logical, coherent, and grammatically correct. Space is limited, so you need to decide what's most important for admissions to know and whether to feature it prominently or less so. Your narrative will help you decide what to include and in what order. It's logical for information most important to you or which shows a major time commitment to be listed first or discussed prominently in essays.

Where to share?

Where you share and how you share is entirely up to you; therefore, your choices will make your application standout positively, negatively, or not at all. A successful application tells a coherent and compelling story about the applicant, so you'll want to share information in the application sections that do that best.

There are seven application sections where you decide what substantive information to share including: honors, activities, essays, guidance counselor recommendation, teacher recommendations, portfolios, and additional information. It's obvious that you'll share your honors and activities in those designated sections, but what about information that isn't an honor or activity? Should you share via essays, guidance counselor recommendation, teacher recommendations, portfolios, or the additional information section? That depends on the type of information you want to share and the impact you want it to have. Suppose you have a high school transcript issue, for example. Underlying every applicant's narrative is that they're a good student, so you'd want to share information to explain such an issue. If it's a simple explanation, then you could write a few sentences explaining it in the additional information section. But what if you'd like some authority to back up your explanation? Then asking your guidance counselor or a teacher to discuss it in their recommendation may be a good idea. As this example shows, there can be strategic reasons to share information in some sections rather than others.

The Honors Section

There is some crossover between honors and activities, e.g., honors that come from activities or vice versa, and you'll have to decide which section to use. Do not duplicate information between your honors and activities sections. Admission officers do not like repetition because it wastes their time. They want to learn something new about you from each part of your application. With that in mind, you may want to consider not listing an honor or activity in order to use it in an essay where admissions can learn something new about you. My kids did that.

- **To make it easier to edit text boxes, use a word processor like WordPad, Word, or Google Docs to edit honors and paste into application text boxes.** Create a brief description, select school/state/regional/national, and the grade level of the honor.
- **If you have a resume that lists your honors, use it for reference to save time.** Make sure that your resume's information matches this section. You'll need a resume for scholarship and college interviews anyway, so you want to make sure that there are no conflicts with your application that could cause confusion.
- **List two honors separated by a comma per slot to fit up to ten.** See example honors section on the next page. The Common Application asks for honors that "are the most meaningful to you" and then provides space for only five. Each of my kids felt like listing up to ten in a logical and concise manner would not test the patience of busy admission officers.
- **Select "Preview" to see what your honors section will look like to admissions.** Once the preview window is open, it provides the option to print. Print the honors section and leave it on your desk for a few weeks to review and make changes.

Which honors should I list and in what order?

List honors most meaningful to you first to last. To keep the list logical, my kids grouped honors by year, so they could list two honors per year. On the next page, for example, please refer to Lauren's honors section from her Common Application that lists eight. Lauren was admitted to Davidson, Duke, and Princeton among others.

Honors

Number 1 GPA Madison High Class of 2020, North Carolina Academic Scholar	School, State/Regional	12
Silver Key Scholastic Art Award 2019 "Goddess of Spring"	State/Regional	11
First Place Science Fair "Road Salt Forest Impact," Teacher Awards Math & Art	School	9
Second Place Science Fair "Disinfectants & Bacteria," Teacher Awards Chemistry & History	School	10
Scholar-Athlete Individual Award NCHSAA	State/Regional	9, 10, 11, 12

Referring to this example, here are a few things to consider when deciding which honors to list and in what order.

- **List accomplishments as honors that are not traditional awards.** If you were honored by or proud of an accomplishment, then it qualifies as an honor regardless of official recognition. For instance, our high school discontinued its valedictorian honor the year Lauren was to graduate, but she listed earning the number one GPA as an honor anyway.
- **If space allows, it's more meaningful and memorable for admissions to read an honor description that includes substantive information about what you did**, so Lauren included titles of her winning art piece and science fair projects. Her artwork was included in an art portfolio submitted with her application where admissions could learn more.
- **Even small honors that you may think insignificant could mean a lot to admissions.** Lauren won four teacher awards in different subjects over two years. Could

admissions conclude that those awards are just as meaningful as teacher recommendations? We thought so.
- **List honors that reinforce your narrative.** Notice that the honors Lauren listed reinforce her narrative: the goat wrangler who caught her braces in a trampoline net and wants to combine art and technology. Her honors reflect art, environmentalism, and acrobatics/athletics, while also reinforcing her ability as a top student.
- **It might make sense to put some of your honors in the activities section instead if they come from activities you list there.** Lauren did that. She had a couple of national awards in taekwondo that she listed with the activity. My sons put their activity awards in the honors section, but put the activities themselves in the activities section without relisting the awards which worked well too. It depends how you decide to organize your application, and where you have space.
- **If you want to list more honors and run out of space, use the additional information section.** Just remember, the application asks you to list the five most important honors to you—not all of them. My kids and I felt that listing ten or less in the honors section would not test the patience of busy admission officers.

The Activities Section

The activities section is one of the most important because it's where admission officers really start to learn why you're special. It therefore deserves a lot of time and attention.

- **To make filling in the text boxes easier, use WordPad, Word, Google Docs to edit your activities and paste into the application text boxes.**
- **If you have a resume that lists your activities, use it for reference to save time.** Make sure that your resume information matches this section. You'll need your resume for scholarship and college interviews, so make

sure that there are no conflicts with your Common Application, e.g., dates and time spent on each activity.
- **Select "Preview" to see what your activities section will look like to admissions.** Once the preview window is open, it gives you the option to print. Print the activities section and leave it on your desk for a few weeks, so you can read it over and make changes.
- **Make sure the time spent on each activity makes sense.** In other words, the amount of time spent on activities is reasonable given the time you spent eating, sleeping, studying, and going to school.

Here are a few things to consider to help you decide which activities to list and their order.

There are ten slots for activities and the application asks, "Please list your activities in the order of their importance to you." List your most meaningful activities first to last. Don't forget interesting hobbies, jobs, or family responsibilities. If there's a specialist or unique activity, all the better! Spiky Ball.

- **The activities you list in the top half of your activities section should be the most important to you and reinforce your application narrative.** If you don't know your narrative yet, return to this section when you do and rearrange, remove, or add to your activities section as needed. See the "Create a Narrative to Focus Your Application" chapter for more.
- **Make sure that the activities which are most important to you make logical sense to be listed first.** For instance, if you're spending the majority of your hours at soccer, cheerleading, or some other activity, it's hard to justify it not being first or at least in the top three. Remember that admissions studies every nuance of your application. If they see that you're spending the lion's share of your time on an activity that's not near or at the top, then they're bound to ask: Why is this applicant spending the majority of their time doing this activity if

it's not meaningful to them? So, take into consideration how much time you spend on an activity when you list it.
- **If a hobby or interest is a major part of your Common Application or supplement essays, consider not listing it in the activities section.** College admission officers want to learn new things about you from each section of your application. That includes the essays. When admission officers read your essays, they'll learn something new about you. My kids did this.
- **If you want to list more activities and run out of space, then use the additional information section.** Just remember, the application provides space for ten activities for a reason. Eiche listed eight activities on his application (admitted University of Virginia, among others), and Max listed nine (admitted Duke). Don't feel pressure to fill all ten slots. It's fine to list less if you spent the majority of your time on fewer pursuits. You should be true to who you are. Authenticity. My kids used the additional information section to elaborate on an activity listed in the activity section, but did not list additional activities. That doesn't mean you shouldn't. If you feel you have important activities yet to list, then list them in the additional information section. Just be careful not to overwhelm and annoy busy admission officers.

How can I maximize space in the activities section?

The activities section is challenging because of the limited space to describe each activity. You have 50 characters for the activity title (about one sentence) and 150 characters for the description (about two sentences). That's not much space to describe the activity, your position/leadership, your accomplishments, recognition, and local/national organization. Always keep in mind that your activity section should be clear and easily understood by admissions. After using these tips, read through your activities section and make sure that your descriptions make sense and are clear. If not, edit them to make them so. Never submit anything in your application that is unclear or not easily understood because it will frustrate busy admission officers. Here are tips to help you get the most out of the space.

- Put as much information as possible in the title. Do not repeat that information in the description.
- Write the descriptions in incomplete sentences as if for a resume.
- Remove spaces when listing items separated by commas or semicolons.
- Use a slash "/ " instead of the word "and" and abbreviate the word "with" as "w/".
- Use "&" in place of the word "and".
- Use initialisms, e.g., Madison High School (MHS).
- Remove punctuation and spaces if doing so does not interfere with meaning or cause confusion.

As an example of how these tips can save you space, please refer to this copy of Lauren's activities section from her application (admitted Davidson, Duke, Princeton among others).

Activities

Athletics: JV/Varsity
Cheerleading, Captain Varsity Team Madison High School (MHS)
Enjoy using skills for MHS spirit:flyer 4yrs.,captain 2yrs.,aerials,handsprings,back tuck.Lead practice,rallies,choreography,banners,fundraisers.

Athletics: Club
Other Sport, Black Belt 2nd Degree Am.TaekwondoFoundation (ATF)
Began age 7. ATF National Black Belt Tournaments: 2017 3rd Forms 5th Sparring;2018 3rd Spar 4th Forms;2019 4th Forms 6th Spar.

Computer/Technology
Java Coding Camp App.State U. & Youth Digital (YD)
Free to 20 students w/Gear Up grant. Design & code Minecraft mods,biomes,tools.YD feedback:Zoo theme,floored at office,best camp mod I have ever seen.

Computer/Technology
Programming/Math Tutor Madison Middle School (MMS)
Invited to tutor Gear Up after-school program in Java. Fun encouraging student creativity. Also tutor in MMS math class during MHS free block.

Environmental
Envirothon CompetitionTeam Wildlife/CEI Specialist
I'm an environmentalist. Learn, laugh, strive with MHS green advocate classmates. 2017 5th FFA State. 2018 3rd FFA State. 2019 tied for 7th Regionals.

Community Service (Volunteer)
Goat Wrangler Carson & Wood Farms
Help local farmers make ends meet by wrangling 60 angora goats for sheering, vaccination. Sort wool for processing. Two days spring/fall.

Community Service (Volunteer)
Camp Eco Madison County Soil & Water District
Environmental camp at Max Patch,Big Bald,Laurel River. Work with US Forest Service/Carolina Mountain Club on trail maintenance/stream cleanup 3 days.

Music: Instrumental
Flautist/Youth Rep.Admin.Council PleasantGapChurch
Learned flute MMS band.Perform Sunday Services.Poll youth/vote church matters.Flautist multi-church:Xmas Tea,Carols & Cookies,Candlelight Xmas Eve.

Community Service (Volunteer)
Flautist Concerts MarsHill/Elderberry/BrooksHowell
Duets/solos with fellow church flautist Carolyn Hamilton at senior communities in spring: PanisAngelicus,L.O.V.E.,KumBaYah,Amazing Grace,Blue Skies.

Athletics: Club
Other Sport, Acrobatics Aerial Space Circus Center
Run away and join the circus for a few hours. Train in lyra, trapeze, and silks. Choreograph and perform routine for summer showcase.

How did Lauren decide to order her list? She dedicated a lot of time to cheerleading earning a leadership position and also to taekwondo earning blackbelts, so she chose them as her top two activities. Given the large time commitments, she felt it wouldn't make sense to do otherwise. In any case, cheer (acrobatics) supported her application narrative: the goat wrangler who caught her braces in a trampoline net and wants to combine art and technology. Computer programming and environmentalism also supported her narrative and were, therefore, listed third through seventh. Although she loves playing the flute, it didn't support her narrative, so she listed it eighth and ninth. Even though circus acrobatics supported her narrative, this activity was such a small commitment that she listed it last. Did you notice there were no art activities in Lauren's activities section? That's because she featured her fascination with art in her Common Application personal essay, so admission officers would learn something new. Strategy.

How to make an impact with the activities section.

- **Have at least one unusual activity**, i.e., a spike. See "A Spiky Ball" chapter for more. In Lauren's case, goat wrangling was a spike and also her third activity Java coding camp where her module received best-in-world recognition. In the additional information section, she elaborated on the camp and recognition. Lauren's guidance counselor also discussed it in her recommendation. Lauren asked her to do that. Strategy.
- **Pick a consistent verb tense to make the section read coherently and flow seamlessly.** Lauren chose present tense because her activities were ongoing. She used past tense when listing something that was clearly over, e.g., "Invited to tutor…". If you decide to use past tense rather than present that's fine, just make sure your tense is consistent throughout the section.
- **Abruptly and briefly change your writing style to make a statement stand out.** Please refer to Lauren's fifth activity "Envirothon CompetitionTeam Wildlife/CEI Specialist". At the beginning of the description, she used a complete sentence: "I'm an environmentalist." She then returned to using resume style incomplete sentences for the rest of the activities section. By changing her style for this one sentence, she made her statement "I am an environmentalist" stand out to make an impact.
- **Weave your personality among the facts, so your voice sings.** In Lauren's activity list, can you see what I mean? Including a few personal comments is like letting in bits of sunlight to illuminate her feelings about her activities. Here are the ones I see:
  -Enjoy using skills for MHS spirit
  -Fun encouraging student creativity
  -I'm an environmentalist

-Learn, laugh, strive with MHS green advocate classmates
-Help local farmers make ends meet
-Panis Angelicus, L.O.V.E., Kumbaya, Amazing Grace, Blue Skies (songs performed)
-Run away and join the circus for a few hours

The Additional Information Section

This section can be used to include just about anything you want admissions to know. It's a good choice, for example, to elaborate on honors/activities or list more. Eiche used it to explain how to pronounce his unusual first name. Lauren used it to explain why she didn't have any teacher recommendations from junior year; her junior classes were dual enrollment not taught by high school staff. Lauren and Max pasted a link to their YouTube art portfolios for colleges that didn't accept portfolios via the Common Application and SlideRoom. You could use this section to paste links to projects, publications, announcements, news articles, or online shop or website you created.

The Future Plans Section

Future Plans is a section that you may want to change depending on where you submit your application. What if you think you want to be an engineer but are unsure, so you apply to a few colleges without engineering schools? Then you probably want to select a non-engineering career interest in future plans for those colleges. Or what if you discover, as Lauren did, that one of your desired majors is in high demand? You may want to select another career interest that's less popular. In Lauren's case, she selected "Computer Science, Bachelors" as her career interest in her early applications. After being deferred by University of Virginia and Duke, she changed it to a less popular major "Artist, Bachelors" for her regular decision applications. Since she wanted to pursue a career involving both computer science and art, she had that flexibility. Strategy.

The Testing Section

Enter SAT, ACT, SAT II and AP scores here. Most top colleges will accept self-reported scores, so you won't have to pay for an official report from a testing agency. If you're admitted and decide to attend, then you'll be required to send an official score report. Check with the colleges to which you're applying to see if they allow self-reported scores.

If you don't have SAT or ACT scores to report due to Covid-19 testing interruptions, you may want to list other scores such as PSAT and/or PreACT in the additional information section (not the Testing section which is meant only for official SAT and ACT scores). Explain your use of PSAT or PreACT scores in the additional information section or your guidance counselor's recommendation. For more discussion about this strategy, please see the "SAT, ACT, SAT II and Test Optional" chapter.

Guidance Counselor & Teacher Recommendations

Most high school students think of their guidance counselor and teacher recommendations as something they have little to no control over. They simply request it via the Common Application, waive their right to read it (FERPA), submit a resume and/or required information form to their counselor and teachers, and then hope for the best. Did you know that you can ask your guidance counselor and teachers to include information in their recommendations that you think is important for colleges to know? You may want to ask them to do that if the information is something related to your high school transcript or activities, and you want your high school's validation. Additionally, if the information is in your guidance counselor's or teacher's recommendation, then it may make a bigger impact than if you put it in the additional information section because admission officers pay close attention to what counselors and teachers say.

Consider, for example, Lauren's situation. As I mentioned a few paragraphs ago, Lauren participated in a Java programming camp in which students programmed Minecraft modules. The company that ran the camp emailed Lauren's school to tell them that her module was the best they'd seen worldwide in three years. Lauren had a copy of the email but struggled to figure out the best way to add this honor to her application. Since the email was received by an administrator in her school district, Lauren asked her guidance counselor to discuss it in her recommendation.

How do you know if your guidance counselor or teacher will actually put the information you request in their recommendation? You don't. That's why it's a good idea to be a little cautious. Since you won't see your recommendations, you won't know for certain. They could forget, get sick, change jobs, or decide not to; though they'd most likely tell you if they decided not to add it. Since you won't know for sure, I suggest that you also add the information in the additional information section just in case. Lauren did that. We thought it wouldn't look redundant to admission officers because they'd think Lauren simply added information without knowing what her guidance counselor discussed in her recommendation.

Art, Music, Writing, Scientific Research, Photography, Architecture and other Application Portfolios

If you're talented, then consider submitting portfolios of your work. A portfolio showcases your talent and growth over time making it a great way to stand out and reinforce your narrative. You'll be able to create one or more portfolios using the Common Application via SlideRoom. Types of portfolios include (but are not limited to) art, music, scientific research (published and unpublished), novels, poetry, news articles, screenplays, performance (vocal, solo, choral, musical instrument, comedy theatre, storytelling), photography, videos, crafting, and building. And the subject matter doesn't necessarily have to support your prospective major. Colleges like to fill their campuses with students that have interests and talents that span departments. For instance, even though Max applied to Duke's Pratt School of Engineering, he submitted an art portfolio. If you have enough quality work in different areas to fill multiple portfolios, then do so. Please be aware that colleges will ask their relevant departments to review your portfolio(s) and evaluate your work.

Chapter Fourteen

Admission Don'ts

"My STEM classes were a disappointment in high school. I need to figure out a way to say that in my essay without hurting anyone's feelings," Eiche explained.

1. Don't throw a teacher, school, guidance counselor, or anyone else under the school bus in your application.

Treat everyone mentioned in your application with dignity and respect. You may be upset about grades or any number of things at your high school, but your college applications are not the place to air those grievances. You may have a situation where things didn't go well, and it wasn't your fault; however, blaming others will only serve to make it look like you can't accept responsibility. There are ways to describe those situations without anger and blame. Eiche confronted this dilemma during his application process. He wanted to discuss the lack of resources at his high school and how some of his classes were a disappointment; however, he was rightly concerned that this could make him look arrogant and ungrateful. This is how he handled it.

Once in high school, I eagerly took chemistry but soon discovered that our science department wasn't as strong as that of larger schools. There are a limited number of advanced courses—no AP chemistry, no calculus. There's limited staff—chemistry and physics are taught by one teacher. Consequently, those classes were not as challenging as I hoped. Moreover, science is unpopular; AP physics has been offered once in the last three years due to lack of interest. I want to attend a university with top-notch facilities where I can immerse myself in chemical engineering surrounded by bright, motivated people who feel the same...

2. Don't leave any unanswered questions in the minds of admission officers.

Review your application and think about any questions you may have left unanswered. Bad grades? Did you move or change schools? Did you start to learn one language and switch to another? Were you sick? How to pronounce your name? Difficult family situation? Economic hardship? Recommendation irregularity? Explain these circumstances in essays, guidance counselor or teacher recommendations, or the additional information section.

3. Don't repeat yourself.

Use each part of your application to show admissions something new about you. They hate repetition because it wastes their time and seems lazy.

4. Don't leave admissions wondering what your future plans and goals are.

It's easy to get so wrapped up in the different parts of your application that you forget future plans. In the Common Application, there's a dropdown menu for future plans (as we discussed in the last chapter) where you can select one major. This is not enough. You need to elaborate elsewhere to give admissions a better idea of your motivation and direction. Providing a sentence or two in an essay is enough. Here are examples of what my kids wrote:

I want to make combining art and technology my life's work. I plan to concentrate my undergraduate studies in art and technology but am eager to explore other opportunities. Last two lines of Lauren's personal essay.

Perhaps I'll become a mechanical, aerospace, biomedical, or computer engineer, artist, some combination, or something else. Second to last line of Max's personal essay.

I want to attend a university with top-notch facilities where I can immerse myself in chemical engineering surrounded by bright, motivated people who feel the same. I need an engineering school with the scope and resources to allow me to discover the part of chemical engineering that I'd like to specialize in, or possibly another field of science that I'd like even more. Second and third to last lines of a supplement essay by Eiche.

5. Don't call or email admissions with questions unless you're the applicant and cannot find the answer on their website or in email.

Some colleges keep track of every email you send and every call you make. Keep that in mind. Also, you need to speak for yourself. Your parents should not be communicating with colleges for you.

6. Don't ignore interview requests.

If you're not going to do an interview, then call or email to let them know.

7. Don't refuse interview requests.

If you do, you will almost certainly not be admitted.

8. Don't post anything on social media that's embarrassing or offensive.

9. Don't forget to proofread your essays and read through your entire application before submitting.

My kids would print out their application to see how it looked in printed form, and also page through the PDF to see how it looked in electronic form.

10. Don't just read your essays—read them aloud!

As you do, change anything that makes you stumble. Your essays should be conversational and flow in such a way that nothing sounds odd or makes you pause. You want admissions focused on your ideas and not on something awkward breaking their focus.

11. Don't leave anything out. No regrets.

Your application is your chance to stand before the admission committee and present yourself for admission. Is there anything you want to say that isn't in the application? This is one of the most important parts of your application process. My kids and I used to say, "No regrets." Meaning, you don't want any. If there's something that you want in your application that isn't there, then find a way to fit it in. Perhaps work it into an essay, the activities or honors section, a portfolio or supplement essay, guidance counselor recommendation, or put it in the additional information section? You want to walk away from the application process feeling like you gave it your all and held nothing back. There will be colleges from which you'll be denied, deferred, or waitlisted. At that moment, you don't want to be wondering if something more could have made a difference. If you give it your all now, then later you'll be at peace knowing you did.

12. Don't wait until the application due date to submit it.

It's simply a good idea to avoid submitting your applications when tens of thousands of people are doing the same. Ideally, submit your applications one or two weeks before the deadline. And if you're not able to do that, then submit it one or two days before the deadline. This will allow you time to fix anything that may go wrong during the submission process. There could be a glitch with the Common or Coalition Application. Or, it may take time for their help team to respond. And if you make a mistake or something is missing, colleges are a lot more willing to work with you if it's before the application deadline.

After you hit "submit," get a good night's sleep. Review your submission again the next day. Did you submit supplements properly? Transcripts? ACT or SAT scores? Portfolios? Recommendations? Watch your email for one from admissions confirming receipt of your application and providing login credentials for your college portal. In your portal, you'll be able to monitor your application checklist and make sure all materials like ACT/SAT scores, transcripts, portfolios, supplements are received by the college. While you await your admission decision, login at least once a week to your portals for any communications from colleges regarding your application and financial aid documents.

Chapter Fifteen

Contacting Admissions: Mistakes, Interviews, Deferrals, Waitlists, and LOCIs

"I just discovered a big mistake." Lauren sighed. Looking defeated, she slumped against my office door. "I submitted the wrong portfolio to Princeton. That's it. I blew it. I'll never get in now."

How to correct a mistake in your submitted application.

Mistakes in grammar or punctuation are too late to fix. What's done is done. If you try to correct it now, you'll only bring their attention to it and make yourself look like you can't roll with a small mistake. However, a large mistake which could have a major impact on the evaluation of your application you must correct. What if you're missing a transcript or submitted something in error? Or, what if you discover that one of your essays is missing a paragraph or key sentence? If it's before the application deadline, then you can be confident that your attempt to correct the problem will be accepted. If it's after the deadline, it may be too late but try anyway. Email your admission officer. Briefly describe the mistake and what you've done to correct it. If your college admission portal has the option to upload into your application file, then create a PDF of your email to admissions and upload it directly into your application file. This way anyone who reviews your application file will see the correction.

Lauren mistakenly submitted an architecture portfolio instead of an art-painting portfolio to Princeton. She realized her mistake about 24 hours after submitting her application. She immediately submitted the correct art-painting portfolio and then emailed Princeton's admission team about the mistake. She also created a PDF of the email and uploaded it into her application file using her

Princeton admission portal. She received a polite email response from admissions confirming receipt of her email but nothing more. Lauren worried right up to Ivy Day that her mistake meant she'd be rejected. She was accepted to Princeton. Everyone makes mistakes. What's important is how you handle them.

What to expect at a college interview.

Most elite colleges offer an alumni interview opportunity. A few weeks after you submit your application, alumni will contact you via email or phone. Interviews are generally low pressure. Pick a coffee shop or other casual, tasteful location to meet. Typically, college interviewers receive basic information about you from admissions like your name, phone number, and a brief list of your interests or intended majors. They don't have access to your application. The interview is an opportunity for you to ask questions about the school and for them to find out what you're like. The alumni interviewer writes a brief email report to admissions about their impressions of you.

How to prepare for your interview.

- Pick a location that is casual but tasteful like a coffee shop.
- A few days before the interview, reread your application essays to remind yourself of your narrative. Your narrative will make it easy for you to describe yourself when you answer the inevitable, "Tell me about yourself?"
- Dress business casual.
- Bring two copies of your resume, so you'll each have one to refer to during the interview. A resume provides the interviewer with information that helps prompt conversation. It also makes you look well prepared and serious about wanting to attend. The facts in your resume should match those in the honors and activities section of your application in case your interviewer sends their copy to admissions and it is compared to your application.

- Research the college and come up with a few questions to ask your interviewer to demonstrate your interest in their school.
- Review anything you're particularly interested in learning about like their abroad programs or curriculum. Lauren did four interviews and the night before each one she studied the campus map to familiarize herself with campus.
- Don't forget to thank your interviewer, and email a follow-up thank you note.

What to do if you're deferred or waitlisted.

If you're deferred EA, ED, REA, or SCEA, or waitlisted RD, you'll have to decide whether you want to continue trying to get in. If so, then you should accept a spot on the deferral or waitlist (sometimes they require you to "opt-in") and begin writing a letter of continued interest (LOCI). A LOCI lets admissions know that you're still interested in attending their college. Timing is important. If deferred, send two LOCIs. One just after the deferral and the second in early January when admissions is considering regular decision candidates. The first LOCI can be somewhat simple. The second should be more detailed and include an additional recommendation. If waitlisted, send one LOCI by mid-April. May 1st is when admissions starts accepting applicants from their waiting list.

How to write a good LOCI.

- Search online for your regional admission officer and email your LOCI directly to them.
- Thank them for considering your application.
- Reaffirm that their college is your first choice.
- Briefly describe what you love about their school.
- Update them with new information about your grades, accomplishments, and honors.
- Add an additional letter of recommendation.

After being deferred by Duke in the ED round, Lauren sent two LOCIs. The first she emailed about a week after her deferral thanking her admission officer for consideration, reaffirming Duke as her first-choice, and discussing what she loved about the school.

Dear ___,

Thank you for reviewing my application to Duke University. Although I was deferred in the early decision round, I want to confirm that Duke remains my first-choice school. I love the energy and enthusiasm of campus, and I was truly impressed by the kind and collaborative spirit of students I met at the Ruby.

I will email you closer to regular decision with an update on my activities and achievements, but please know that I am still committed to Duke.

Thank you again.

Her second LOCI was sent in January so that it would be in her application file when reviewed alongside regular decision candidates. It updated her GPA, honors, accomplishments and included an additional recommendation.

Dear ___,

I want to thank you and your office for the time and consideration put into my application. Although my ED application was deferred for regular decision consideration, Duke remains my top choice, and I would very much like to be admitted; therefore, I wish to update you on my achievements.

In January, I participated in the Scholastic Art Awards competition and received a silver key for my eight-piece, climate change inspired, watercolor portfolio "Metanoia." ...

I also received a couple more pieces of information that I hope will strengthen my application. Upon completion of first semester, my weighted GPA increased from 4.562 to a 4.574, and

I learned that my cheer team had the highest average GPA of varsity teams at my high school. Additionally, I was honored to receive the MVP award from my cheerleading coach. Coach ___ awards MVP to one senior on the varsity team each year. As captain of the team, I lead practices, organize pep rallies and fundraisers, choreograph routines, and design t-shirts. I asked Coach ___ to write a supplemental letter of recommendation that addresses my role within the team. Please find her letter attached to this email.

Thank you for your continued consideration of my application.

Lauren was admitted to Duke regular decision. Unfortunately for Duke, she was also admitted to Princeton which was beyond her wildest dreams.

Chapter Sixteen

Application Disasters

"Rewatch your YouTube art portfolio and look more carefully at the patches on your backpack," I warned. Lauren whipped out her phone. "Oh no! Do you think they've seen it yet?"

Failure stings, but there's also humor in those face-palm moments particularly in hindsight. I'm glad my kids put it all out there and gave it their best shot. When you risk a lot, you can take a hard fall. But if you don't shoot for the stars, you're certain to never reach them. No regrets. Just hearty laughs over stupid mistakes. This is a blooper reel. Enjoy.

Submitted an art portfolio to University of North Carolina Chapel Hill which contained a "Forever Duke" pin

No college wants to see your love for another in their application. That's especially true when the two universities are the University of North Carolina Chapel Hill and Duke. The schools are practically neighbors with campuses eight miles apart. And UNC-Duke is one of the most famous rivalries in college sports. You'd think Lauren would be extra careful when applying to these two schools? LOL

Carolina doesn't accept art portfolios via SlideRoom, so Lauren created a YouTube portfolio and pasted the link in the additional information section of her UNC Common Application. About 48 hours after submission, I was watching her YouTube art portfolio video and noticed a "Forever Duke" pin on her backpack pinned among patches she'd made. Omg! How could this have happened? The pin was a gift from her older brother and Duke student Max. She completely forgot it was on her backpack. Had UNC admissions seen it yet? Since it was still before the application deadline, we thought probably not. She knew that she needed to fix this fast—but how? Should she delete the video and make a new one? No, if she did that then the link to her art portfolio in her application wouldn't work. Could she email UNC admissions a new link? Yes, but she didn't want to bother them. How about editing the video to remove the image? If she did that, then UNC wouldn't see her exquisite patches with meaningful messages. After some playing around with YouTube's editor, Lauren discovered that she could blur the image of the "Forever Duke" pin without affecting the patches. LOL disaster averted. And yes, Lauren was admitted to both UNC (early action) and Duke (regular decision).

Applied to colleges we couldn't afford

Imagine applying to seven colleges only to discover that you can't afford five of them? That's what happened to Eiche. He was the first in our family to apply to college and my first time as coach. He was accepted to seven schools and five of them we couldn't afford. We didn't realize our mistake until his financial aid offers came out. Luckily, he received low-income waivers for his application fees; still, it was heartbreaking to watch him say no to schools he'd fallen in love with. Plus, how about all the time and effort spent on those applications and college visits? Ouch. For more about this mistake and how to avoid it, see the "You Can Afford It. Need Blind vs Meet Full Need" chapter.

Failure to research dooms application

For years, Lauren dreamt of attending Duke University. When she was deferred in Duke's early decision round, she had just two weeks to apply regular decision to other schools. The colleges she selected were Harvard, Cornell, and Princeton. She quickly researched them focusing on her intended majors, beauty of campus, and study abroad programs. She also grappled with a crisis of confidence. Although she was admitted early action to UNC and NC State, she believed her deferral by Duke meant that her application was not as strong as it could be. Would a change in strategy help? She'd applied to her early round schools as a computer science major with a minor in art. I'd been hanging out in college forums reading posts and articles about colleges expanding their facilities to accommodate a flood of computer science majors. In fact, many forum posts advised not to apply as computer science because the popularity of the major could hurt admission chances. After discussing the pros and cons, Lauren decided to change strategy by applying to her regular decision schools as an art major with a computer science minor.

About a week before Ivy Day, I discovered that applying to Cornell as fine arts rather than computer science was a big mistake. I was researching what the acceptance rate was for kids like Lauren who applied to Cornell's College of Architecture, Art, and Planning and discovered that their fine arts department was extremely selective with only a few undergraduate fine arts majors. Lauren had practically no chance of being admitted with that major. Her chance of admission would have been much greater if she'd applied as a computer science major to either the college of arts and sciences or the college of engineering. We realized a week before Ivy Day that she would be rejected by Cornell. It taught us a tough but good lesson—always thoroughly research the college to which you apply. Her Ivy Day results: Cornell-rejected, Harvard-rejected, Princeton-admitted, Duke-admitted.

An F off

The prompt from the University of Virginia asked: "What work of art, music, science, mathematics, or literature has surprised, unsettled, or challenged you, and in what way?" One of Lauren's favorite artworks is "The Great Wave Off Kanagawa" by Katsushika Hokusai, so she picked it as her essay topic. Unfortunately, she thought the piece was titled "The Great Wave of Kanagawa" and wrote her essay accordingly. She was an "f" off. Now, this error may not be as bad as it seems because the artwork is widely known by other names such as: "Under the Wave off Kanagawa," "The Great Wave," and "The Wave." Regardless, she should have realized her mistake especially since she looked up the piece on the Web to learn how to spell Hakusai's name. The correct title was right there in front of her, but she didn't notice. About a month after submitting her application, Lauren realized her mistake. Hoping UVa admissions might not notice the error or care even if they did, she decided not to email them to correct it. UVa deferred her early action and then waitlisted her in the regular decision round.

Odds parent pressure

When Max applied to Duke early decision (ED), his fallback plan was to apply to Vanderbilt University early decision two (ED2) if deferred or denied by Duke. Since he was accepted ED to Duke, he didn't execute that plan. As I've mentioned, Lauren also dreamt of Duke; however, she had no interest in going to Vanderbilt. When Duke deferred her, she refused to apply to Vanderbilt ED2 (20% admit rate) even though the chances of getting into Duke or an Ivy League university regular decision were below 6%. "What if Vanderbilt says yes, and then I have to go?" Lauren worried. LOL A textbook case of someone who should not be applying ED or at all! The minute she said that I realized it didn't matter how much better the odds were of getting into Vanderbilt; she shouldn't apply. Luckily, she got in regular decision to three schools she loved—Davidson, Duke, and Princeton. My husband and I put a fair amount of pressure on Lauren to apply to Vanderbilt ED2 because we loved the school. Lauren said no and went her own way. Lesson learned: Applicants should follow their heart regardless of odds or parent pressure.

Help People Like You Beat the System!

Please write a book review for this book on Amazon. The only way people who need this book will find it is with Amazon reviews. Let me explain why.

First, thank you for reading my book. I hope it helps you navigate the college admission process. When I started coaching my kids, we didn't have much money. I spent hundreds of hours learning about the process because we didn't have the advantages that wealthy families enjoy such as consultants, prep courses, legacy, private or affluent high school and the like. I have to confess that I was and still am a little angry that it is so difficult to learn this important information. That's why I wrote this book—to make it available at an affordable price to everyone applying to college who wants it. The only way more families will learn about this book and how it can help their kids get into and afford their dream schools is through reviews on Amazon. Reviews raise the book's ranking so it shows up in Amazon searches when people search for help with college admission or applications. That means that when you write a review, you're helping this important information get out to people like you who really need it! Please take a few minutes and leave a review. I read every one of my reviews. I honestly want to know how the book helped you and where I can improve to make things clearer.

Thank you again! —Elizabeth Gardner aka Coach Mom

About the Author

Attorney turned award-winning author Elizabeth Gardner has been providing practical and effective parenting strategies since 2002. Her books *Crib Sheets New Parent Sleep Solutions* and *Canny Granny How to Be the Favorite Grandparent* were awarded Mom's Choice Awards® for outstanding parenting books in 2010.

   Her latest book *Coach Mom Top College Admission Playbook* (2021) and successful Coach Mom Instagram, TikTok, and YouTube help thousands of high school students get into their dream schools. A budget-conscious mom coach of three teens admitted to top colleges including the Ivy League, coach mom Elizabeth Gardner reveals successful application strategy secrets. Perfect for the high school applicant or parent coach, *Coach Mom Top College Admission Playbook* guides you every step of the way to create compelling applications that stand out. Elizabeth lives a happy, quiet life in Weaverville, North Carolina.

Made in the USA
Coppell, TX
22 July 2022